Violent Democracy

This fascinating and provocative book will change the way you think about democracy. Challenging conventional wisdom, Daniel Ross shows how violence is an integral part of the democratic system from its origins and into its globalised future. He draws on the examples of global terrorism and security, the wars in Iraq and Afghanistan, the relation of colonial powers to indigenous populations, and the treatment of asylum seekers. His analysis of these controversial issues moves beyond the comfortable stances of both left and right to show that democracy is violent, from its beginning and at its heart.

Daniel Ross is one of Australia's rising intellectuals. He recently obtained a doctorate in political science from Monash University, under the title "Heidegger and the Question of the Political." He is also co-director of the recent film *The Ister*.

"This highly topical book examines how democracies are trying to cope with the potentially endless war on terrorism. The author argues that the origin and heart of democracy is essentially violent and that the threat of terrorist attack is not only exposing new forms of 'democratic violence' but could transform the very character of the democracies we seek to defend. Do we have the right, for example, to bring democracy to others by force? A revealing and disturbing work that every democratic leader should study while there is still time." – Phillip Knightley

Violent Democracy

Daniel Ross

CAMBRIDGE
UNIVERSITY PRESS

PUBLISHED BY THE PRESS SYNDICATE OF THE UNIVERSITY OF CAMBRIDGE
The Pitt Building, Trumpington Street, Cambridge, United Kingdom

CAMBRIDGE UNIVERSITY PRESS
The Edinburgh Building, Cambridge, CB2 2RU, UK
40 West 20th Street, New York, NY 10011– 4211, USA
477 Williamstown Road, Port Melbourne, VIC 3207, Australia
Ruiz de Alarcón 13, 28014 Madrid, Spain
Dock House, The Waterfront, Cape Town 8001, South Africa

http://www.cambridge.org

First published by Cambridge University Press 2004

Printed in Australia by Ligare Pty Ltd

Typefaces Minion 11/13 pt., Helvetica and StrayHorn   *System* LaTeX 2_ε [TB]

A catalogue record for this book is available from the British Library

National Library of Australia Cataloguing in Publication data

Ross, Daniel, 1970–.
Violent democracy.
Bibliography.
Includes index.
ISBN 0 521 60310 2.
1. Democracy.   2. Political violence.   3. War on Terrorism, 2001–.
4. Political refugees.   5. Indigenous peoples – Colonization.   I. Title.
303.6

ISBN 0 521 60310 2 paperback

For Ezra

Contents

Introduction   *page* 1

1 The High Horse and the Low Road   14
2 Strangers in a Familiar Land   36
3 Sorry We Killed You   59
4 The Great Debate   80
5 Border Protection and Alien Friends   104
6 Enemy Combatants   124
  Afterword: The Politics of Torture   151

Notes   174
References   179
Index   181

Introduction

A new Fascism, with its trail of intolerance, of abuse, and of servitude, can be born outside our country and be imported into it, walking on tiptoe and calling itself by other names, or it can loose itself from within with such violence that it routs all defenses. At that point, wise counsel no longer serves, and one must find the strength to resist. Even in this contingency, the memory of what happened in the heart of Europe, not very long ago, can serve as support and warning.   *Primo Levi*[1]

Since its invention democracy has imagined itself as the solution to the violence of tyranny and chaos. But democracy has from the beginning contained its own potential for violence, for instance the violence of capitalism. This is not only the violence of economic or imperial wars, but also the consequence of opening and penetrating both consumer and labor markets. More generally there is violent power involved in the fluidity of capital, which can enrich or impoverish one state or another with drastic results. Even on its own terms, democracy has reserved the right to resort to violent action and claimed a monopoly on the "legitimate" use of violent means. The legitimacy of this monopoly has always been dependent upon the assertion of just ends. Violent means were always relative to and justified on the grounds of democratic *ends*, even when democracy perpetrated deadly violence.

With the advent of the War on Terror comes a reorganization of these concepts, a shift away from democratic ends, and towards the *self*-justification of violent means. In the concept and reality of *terrorism* those states that refer to themselves as democracies are discovering a new potentiality for violence and are resolutely and

1

confidently granting themselves a new right to act on it. Democratic states are re-assessing the situation of the world, with conclusions that affect democracy more profoundly than did the great wars of the twentieth century. Those earlier wars were grasped as aberrant conditions caused by a specific threat, requiring temporary sacrifices in order to defeat the enemy. Democratic sacrifices were thus only conditional, on the implicit promise that they would be reversed when the threat was overcome.

The War on Terror is formulated as a potentially endless struggle against an infinitely extended enemy, that permeates all borders, and that may inhabit any sphere. The new situation is essentially militarized, the sovereignty of individual states less important than a coordinated and integrated system of "security." Such a system may be centralized in the United States, but nevertheless implies the creation of planetary security arrangements that transcend any particular state. The development of such a system of security produces its own means, logic and autonomy, unlimited by the concept of state sovereignty.

In such a situation democracy becomes merely one value among others, a *preference*, but potentially and perpetually deferrable. Thus the risk is that the violence in question will turn out to be against the very possibility of democracy, at least as it has been understood until now. In the *new* state of democracy, old authoritarian tendencies are transformed into new ways and means, new laws and powers, new techniques of surveillance and control, new spaces and forms of imprisonment or homicide, that redefine the essence of the state itself. The state ceases to be the form through which the citizenry freely and politically, singly and collectively, make their lives. It becomes, rather, one mechanism within the overall system dedicated to the security and survival of the populace.

These new forms of violence not only demonstrate the "reaction" to terror, but equally show a capacity *already* contained within "democracy" itself. Even if democracy is being transformed or undermined, this is occurring, significantly, in the context of a *continuation* of the "democratic system" itself. There is, therefore, a dual origin to these new forms of violence, an origin in the character of the present situation, and an origin in the political system itself. Understanding what is presently occurring, therefore, is not only a matter of following the latest developments, but of grasping the essence of democracy in its foundations, even or especially where these foundations may be in the process of being undone.

Two thoughts underlie this book. The first is that the origin and heart of democracy is essentially violent. The second is that our present situation is revealing new forms of the violent potential of democracy, and that this is presently transforming the character of the "democracies" we inhabit. Each chapter follows a different way in which these two thoughts may be articulated together.

Violence

Any act of force or power can be described as violent. "Violence" means action forceful enough to produce an effect. A violent storm is one that leaves behind its marks. These marks are the disorder and destruction that wind and rain have the power to cause. Violence is thus something physical, something that affects things in the world.

When one imagines violence, however, what first springs to mind is not the *source* of violence, but that *against which* it acts. Before thinking of physical forces, one thinks of actions committed against *bodies*, living beings. Violence is first of all something done *to* bodies, human and animal. Violence against plant life is also certainly possible, yet it is unlikely that this is the kind of violence anyone first thinks of.

Violence is something done to bodies. Those actions are violent that leave *marks*. It is possible to commit violence that leaves no visible mark, but in this case the marks are internal. Or else what is marked is the *experience* of the person or animal that has suffered violence. Their experience is marked by the sensation of pain.

Perhaps there is no touching without some violence. Might all contact leave its mark on the body, or on the experience of the one whose body it is? Leaving a mark means having an effect, changing something. If this is not always a matter of damage or injury, it is nevertheless a power or force. All touch involves some kind of force, of one body upon another, of *something* that contacts some body.

Not all bodies are human or animal, or even vegetable. There are celestial bodies and bodies of water. Every thing that can be isolated from other things is susceptible to being described as a body. The idea of the body implies a *whole*, something whole within itself. A body is contained within its boundaries, its surface, or its skin. It occupies a certain space. That "violence" means to mark or affect a body, to damage or injure a body, suggests that the whole is affected by something outside it.

Violence usually implies a *rupturing* of the surface of a body, a wound. In requiring some kind of mark, even an internal or experiential mark, violence implies some kind of penetrative force, something that breaks through and inscribes an effect. Thus, even though the concept of a body implies a whole, the possibility of violence means that this whole must be *susceptible* to penetration. Violence means that what is supposedly closed within its boundaries, its surface or its skin, is able to be opened.

There are also political bodies, bodies of knowledge, and closed systems of thought. The concept of violence equally applies to these bodies. Violence in this sense means some kind of rupturing or breaking into. Again, the possibility of violence implies that what was grasped as a whole is *susceptible* to something else, to something *beyond* its bounds. In order for this to be possible, the whole must *already* exist in relation to what lies outside it. Otherwise it would be impervious to any force. So long as the possibility of violence remains, wholeness cannot be absolute.

Cancer might be understood as violence that does not require any penetration. But the wholeness of the body is still undermined by cancer. Instead of functioning as a closed system, as something self-contained, the body is rendered an improper whole. The whole fails to function as a whole, and the consequence is violence perpetrated against the body by itself. The body wounds and penetrates itself from inside. Political bodies and bodies of thought are susceptible to this kind of violence too.

Democracy

Democracy was discovered or invented by the Greeks. Its birth was both difficult and complex. Those who *rejected* democracy as the *poorest* form of governance, for example, may have coined the term. Democracy meant the rule of everybody and hence nobody, the abdication of the responsibility to place government in the hands of the best. No single great mind conceived democracy, nor was it the outcome of one momentous decision of the Athenian body politic. Each of the uncertain steps toward democracy was a *response* to a period of disorder or tyranny. The most important of these intermediary steps were achieved by non-democratic decisions to *grant* one person – Solon, Cleisthenes – the power to implement reforms. These founding heroes of Greek democracy were able to implement those reforms the Athenian public recognized were beyond its ability.

The birth of *modern* democracy was equally complex. Like Greek democracy, modern democracy was born less in theory than in struggle. Or, rather, out of a complex interrelation of the two. Most importantly, the evolution of modern democracy coincided with the diminution of monarchical sovereignty grounded in divine right. The replacement of monarchical sovereignty with a sovereignty grounded in the people is usually understood as a radical political transformation. This is the fable modern democracy tells of its origins.

The fundamental continuity between these conceptions of sovereignty is less frequently attended to. But in many ways the transition from monarchy to democracy involved the reconfiguring of religious sovereignty on a secular basis, a translation rather than a transformation. The most succinct formulation of this thought was Carl Schmitt's statement that all significant concepts of the modern theory of the state are secularized theological concepts.[2]

The essence of modern democracy is the thought that the ground of sovereignty is the people themselves. That is, the only legitimate basis for instituting any system of political decision-making and any system of law is the will of the people to do so. This, it should be noted, is not only the ground of Western representative democracy. It is just as certainly the ground of Soviet, Chinese, or North Korean communism, and even of German National Socialism.

In all these cases the legitimacy of the politico-juridical system lies entirely with the will of the people, rather than any being that transcends the people. Even in Nazi Germany the rule of the Führer was based in the will of the people, in spite of the fact that this will was not determined through any political process, and that the voicing of dissent was prohibited. The will was transmitted, according to the Nazi mythology, *directly* from the people to the

Führer and vice versa, yet the ground of sovereignty resided wholly with the *Volk*.

This exposes the breadth of democracy grasped as the sovereignty of the people. This definition is therefore usually further limited, requiring, say, freedom of speech, the separation of powers, or representative elections. Such definitional requirements make the concept of democracy more specific, and are the means by which democrats convince themselves that democracy is the antithesis of fascism and totalitarianism.

By restricting the definition of democracy, however, its proponents inhibit the exploration of its theoretical foundations. The price paid for this inhibition is an inability to address the strange impossibility of democracy, or to see where its foundations might overlap with the foundations of other political systems, or to pursue the relationship between its philosophical ground and the manner of its unfolding in practice.

"Democracy," then, signifies a concept with several layers. *Firstly*, "democracy" signifies those states in which the citizenry elect some form of representative parliament, in which the separation of the executive, legislative, and judicial powers is embraced, and which on these grounds refer to themselves *as* "democracies." *Secondly*, "democracy" refers to that fundamental concept of the sovereignty of the people. In this case the broadest possible conception of sovereign democracy is intended, excluding neither communism nor fascism. The context in each case hopefully reduces the risk of confusing these differing meanings.

But there is a *third* understanding of the meaning of "democracy" operating in the text. This third meaning only occasionally surfaces explicitly, but underlies much of the discussion. Both the first two meanings of democracy are grounded in the concept of sovereign rule. And this means, in an understanding that democracy is a *system*, a process or procedure or law, based in the will of the people, *organizing* that will and standing independently of it.

Politics always includes the possibility of disruption. Understanding democracy as a closed system eliminates what makes it political. It is to imagine the democracy of political philosophers, rather than the democracy of struggle. It is to see democracy as the system *already* instituted and implemented, rather than as a political *force*, a possibility still to come, *potentially threatening* whatever currently is. If the will of the people is understood as always capable of new forms, then it can never be *finally and eternally* settled in any system or constitution. However successful they may be, institutions and constitutions always contain the possibility that it will be discovered they are utterly *wrong*. Democracy is, then, a constant possibility, directed toward the future, a potential threat to any political whole, and a kind of promise.[3]

Democracy has a violent heart

The first thought underlying this book is that the origin and heart of democracy is essentially violent. By "democracy" is meant any political system grounded in the idea that sovereignty lies with the people. By "violence" is meant, more than anything else, that which ruptures a body. Democracy is violent because in its origin it breaks into reality in a way that is beyond containment within any closed system of thought.

Founding democracy is always violent because it gives what it does not have. The decision that the people shall be the ground of a new sovereignty is never a decision the people can take themselves. If a declaration founds a new law, it cannot rely upon any previously established sovereignty on which to base an idea of the people. The declaration to found a democracy is always the pronouncement that "we, the people" *are*. Democracy is never the sovereignty of *all* people, but rather the sovereignty of the people of *this* democracy. And *these* people *are* a people only by way of the declaration itself. The declaration gives "a people" that it does not have.

The people are invented in the declaration that founds democracy. Or, to put it another way, the declaration of a democracy establishes a *border*, the border that divides those included and those excluded from what is founded. In short, the declaration can never itself be a democratic act. The declaration is a promise that the people will be, the border will be, and the democracy will be. Yet the declaration also *presupposes* that there is a people, that there is a legitimate border separating those within and those outside the democracy-to-be.

Thus, strictly speaking, the foundation of democracy is impossible. That acts of declaration have founded "democracies" can hardly be denied. But it is never certain, at the moment of foundation, that what has been founded is truly democratic. Perhaps nothing is ever really and truly democratic. Yet the concept of democracy demands that no sovereignty is legitimate if it is not the sovereignty of the people. Democracies, therefore, should never be able to rest comfortably in the thought that democracy never wholly exists.

The uncertainty of the act of foundation provokes the need for further confirmation of democracy's legitimacy. This need for further confirmation is itself marked in the forms and ways of existing democracies. That in many democratic states the head of state must sign each new government into existence is one of these marks. The head of state is that sovereign authority whose signature inscribes the legitimacy of each democratic decision. Yet the final confirmation of the legitimacy of democratic sovereignty is never forthcoming.

Democracy is violent, then, because it can never form a closed system. Founded on the violent claim that "here, now" democracy has begun, a "democracy" continues to carry this violence at its heart. But this lack of closure, this wound on the democratic body, is not easily tolerated. Democracy tells itself that of course it is indeed democratic, and is prepared to stake its existence on this fact. Democracy cannot *openly* "*know*" its originary violence, but this violence continues to determine the paths a democracy follows. This ongoing determination is on the one hand a matter of certain structural features of democratic systems. But it is not only a structural matter. That democracy cannot admit the violence at its origin also means that this origin continues to *haunt* everything that follows it.

The ongoing violence of democracy, then, is not just *any* violence, not just the fact that the police carry batons. Yet all enforcement of law is a manifestation of the need for law to *inscribe* itself on the political body. The violence of democracy is also that originary violence without which specific instances of democracy could not have been inaugurated. It is the massacre of indigenous populations, or the crushing of those who oppose a new foundation of the people's sovereignty. And it is the ongoing history of forgetting this original violence, not out of spite or indifference, but because the violence at the origin of democracy threatens democracy itself.

The new state of democracy

The second thought underlying this book is that the violence of democracy has changed, or is unfolding in a certain direction, across the twentieth and into the twenty-first centuries. Something is in the process of emerging, awaiting our understanding. It is not merely that violence is increasing. Of course, the wars of the twentieth century were the bloodiest in history, and throughout that century millions were slaughtered in the name of the people's will. Although the technological means for producing such slaughter continues inexorably to advance, *especially* in those countries that call themselves democracies, the violence of war ebbs and flows. Measured by the quantity of corpses, the Gulf Wars were placid affairs in comparison with the Vietnam War. And the most advanced weaponry is hardly necessary to achieve the most brutal results, as the Rwandan catastrophe so amply illustrated.

For most of its existence modern democracy has conceived itself as a stable system. In *earlier* centuries war and conquest formed part of the very *raison d'être* of a state, and peacetime was more akin to a re-gathering of strength in readiness for the next campaign. All modern democracies continue to prepare in case of war. But unlike earlier democracies, modern democracies have mostly regarded war as an occasionally necessary aberration, rather than something essential to the life of a democracy.

This detachment of the life of the modern state from its military capacity has determined the way in which democracy relates to law. The difference between military and police is the distinction between conceptions of law. Military rule implies that power emanates directly from the sovereign, a matter of might and fact. The power of a police force is only *indirectly* related to the sovereign. Law stands independently of that sovereignty, as shown by the legitimate *right* of the law or the police to act *even against* the sovereign. That the law is autonomous implies it is conceived as *transcendent*, as permanent and eternal. The *norms* of law, grounded in the sovereignty of the people and the dignity of humanity, are essentially inviolable.

The twentieth century is divided into two halves by the extermination of the Jews in Europe. This was not merely another wartime massacre on a larger scale, but the decision to systematically eradicate an entire population, with whatever industrial means best facilitated the outcome. Although the 1942 Wannsee conference took place in wartime the decision was not a military one, but rather partook of another, more enigmatic, logic. Yet although the decision was not military or strategic, this logic was unlike any normal peacetime legislation, founded as it was upon the designation of an absolute *enemy*.

The decision to implement the "Final Solution" was a singular event. But the entire apparatus by which from 1933 onward the Jews were transported and corralled, controlled, degraded, and finally killed, was equally singular. From the systematic way in which National Socialism stripped the Jews of all rights, to the complex and calculated arrangements through which it dehumanized and murdered them in the camps, it deployed a remarkable array of means with which to "treat" this "enemy." Thereby National Socialism revealed a single-minded determination to carry out its will, exceeding all barriers of law or humanity.

Those victims of this will not only suffered violent treatment. They were thoroughly, gradually, and systematically divested of all those qualities with which humanity convinces itself of its dignity and the justness of its sovereignty. This scar on humanity, of course, left its imprint not only upon the victims, but equally upon those capable of devising and carrying out such acts.

The second half of the twentieth century was marked by the violence of the extermination. These marks were left, for instance, in the formation and political history of Israel. They were left in the collective psychology of the German people, as shame or the refusal of shame, as the ability or inability to mourn for the lost Germany. And they were left in the legal systems of various democracies and international juridical bodies. They were left, for instance, in the concept of "crimes against humanity."

The name itself, "crime against humanity," exposes that it is a reaction, a wish to *save* the transcendent concepts of law and humanity from this event. It is the very culmination and last resort of the idea of law grounded in the sovereignty of humanity. But if it is such, it is so out of desperation, out of the fear and perhaps the knowledge that what was fatally damaged by the extermination was the notion of transcendent law grounded in human dignity. Such is the conclusion of Giorgio Agamben:

This is also why Auschwitz marks the end and the ruin of every ethics of dignity and conformity to a norm. The bare life to which human beings were reduced neither demands nor conforms to anything. It itself is the only norm; it is absolutely immanent. And "the ultimate sentiment of belonging to the species" cannot in any sense be a kind of dignity.[4]

If this is so, then the concept of "crimes against humanity" is not only the last resort of law grounded in human sovereignty. It is also the symptom of the inability to locate any other ground for law or politics. The sixty years since the extermination are then comprehensible as the consequences of denial, a denial of the degree to which the basis of democratic thinking has been undone by this singular event. And with this denial, even in its perpetual call to never forget, the work of forgetting advances.

In more recent times, however, a different logic is making itself visible in the workings of democracy. This logic is increasingly prepared to dispense with the concepts of transcendent law and humanitarianism. One source of this new logic is the recognition that if capitalism is in fact a planetary economic and technical system, then it has its own requirements, which exceed the laws of each nation. A process of unwinding national sovereignty has thus been underway for some time, reducing democracies to local councils, with powers limited by global competition and by transnational bodies regulating economic and other matters.

This global process has sometimes produced political consequences that undermine it. As sovereignty appears to wither, the citizenry of democracies reacts, rationally and irrationally. Governments are elected that resist the pressures of globalization, or that are committed to strengthening national sovereignty, national identity, and national borders. The processes of globalization have until now had to *cope* with democracy, coercing and managing it, but occasionally stymied by determined electorates.

The largest democracies, however, have managed to advance their integration into a global system without substantial public interference, and without overtly sacrificing the instruments of democracy, such as free speech or representative elections. What is remarkable about today's freedom of speech is its inverse correlation with the visibility of dissent. Freedom of speech increasingly means freedom of entertainment. The electoral system itself becomes one more form of entertainment, subsumed to the needs of the media system. The distance from Athens to Washington is thereby revealed.

If the violence of democracy has changed, it is not only a matter of punitive or overt violence. The violence inherent to the "benevolent" operations of the state upon its citizenry, that is, in matters of health and welfare, must also be recognized. The state increasingly organizes and penetrates the bodies of its populace, either to "optimize" the functioning and survival of the individual or of the state itself. The body of the citizenry is increasingly available to the state as *matter*, to be controlled, stimulated, improved, treated, manipulated, harvested or terminated.

Since 11 September 2001, however, something else has emerged, in the United States, England, Australia, and elsewhere. It is not so much war that has changed, but the way in which democracy imagines itself. "Democracy" seems to be rethinking itself, no longer on the ground of transcendent law based in the sovereignty of a people. Law is reconfigured on the basis that there is an enemy, internal and external, against which it is necessary to *act* rather than react. The law thus becomes that *weapon* for seeking out and hunting down those enemies that threaten "democracy." The exigencies of the new situation increasingly undermine the constraining effect upon governments and legislators played by notions of legal rights and human dignity. Law is reconceived on a war footing. Or, more precisely, and resembling Nazism, peacetime and wartime, and right and fact, are increasingly convergent.

It is remarkable that this re-imagination of democracy occurred at precisely the moment when globalization seemed to suggest that war had finally become anachronistic and inexpedient. Yet if this is the return of a martial sovereignty, it is not simply a matter of the authoritarianism of military dictatorship. It is, more complexly, the falling away of the notion that law transcends the bare facts of human life, that law responds to and *confers* the dignity of humanity. It is the final evaporation of the thought that the political life is part of the essence of humanity.

Rather, men and women are simply those beings that inhabit the system that protects them, the system in which they work and consume, in which they are kept healthy, and in which they die. If dignity remains a relevant concept in this new democracy, it may take the nostalgic form of the honor and discipline of the protective and valorous guardians. The new hero of democracy is the military and intelligence machine dedicated to detecting and thwarting the work of the enemy terrorist.

But the new state of democracy is not merely a militarized one, but a hybrid of martial logic and medical/managerial technocracy. The response to the post-11 September American anthrax scare exemplifies the convergence of "health" and "defense," with hospitals forced to stockpile medicines in case of a terrorist catastrophe. More importantly, hospitals were forced to re-imagine their function in terms of the overall scheme of "homeland security." Conversely, military personnel are coerced to take "protective" drugs to guard against the possibility of biological, chemical, or nuclear attack. Human beings are the material of the state, to be protected from internal and external enemies, *and* to be protected from suffering, disease, and death, by an ostensibly democratic, human, and benevolent authority, but one that is equally autocratic, inaccessible, medico-technical, and capable of powerful controlling and destructive violence.

This new state of democracy no longer has the sovereignty of the people or the dignity of humanity at its core. For this reason, it may also be the means by which the future of the state is reconciled with the process of globalization. The dangers of these developments are obvious, comprising dangers to the rights of individuals, to the concept of life, and to democracy itself. But transcendent law and human dignity were in some way veils concealing difficult truths about human existence, truths exposed at Auschwitz. First among them is that law and dignity are impotent and false when confronted with the worst. If this is accepted, then at least what was concealed may become visible. On the other hand, democracy *may* be the name and the guise under which the worst returns. Perhaps the way of thinking that made the camps possible continues to work its effects and is even resurgent. If democracy has a future meaning other than as the vehicle of a new and unprecedented fascism, it must be reinvented, such that it again gains the possibility of rupture, of disrupting the reality of what is currently violently unfolding itself.

Chapter 1

The High Horse and the Low Road

Reports that say that something hasn't happened are always interesting to me, because as we know, there are known knowns; there are things we know we know. We also know there are known unknowns; that is to say, we know there are some things we do not know. But there are also unknown unknowns – the ones we don't know we don't know. And if one looks throughout the history of our country and other free countries, it is the latter category that tend to be the difficult ones.   *Donald Rumsfeld*

I think we agree, the past is over.   *George W Bush*

That George Herbert Walker Bush's little boy grew up to himself become president of the United States of America was the result of a peculiar sequence of corporate fundraising, campaign spectacle, votes received, technological failure and, finally, legal determination. Whether the final outcome was actually "democratic" was questioned at the time. This doubt was only compounded by the fact that, in the legal judgment that settled the Bush presidency, it was explicitly stated that the ruling applied *in this case only*, and established no legal precedent. But, in spite of the objections of Al Gore and his supporters, there was little evidence of either public antipathy or joy for the legal decision proclaiming Bush victor. Throughout the Florida process – which might be referred to synecdochically as the saga of the Hanging Chad – there was little sense that much was at stake beyond the personal fortunes of the candidates. Although the peccadilloes and style of the Clinton presidency may have provoked deep resentment in Republican Congressmen, this never translated into any serious division within the American public. While there were those who cared passionately about Gore versus Bush, for most the decision was akin to an entertainment spectacle, on par with the question of Leno versus Letterman. Since the public has learnt that campaign policy promises are empty rhetoric, there was little to separate the candidates. For most the question of who was the most telegenic was as important as any, since the victor would be filling screens for the next four years. If this was democracy, then it took a form that was highly attenuated from any public participation.

It is difficult to avoid the feeling that, in spite of a fairly regular alternation between Democrat and Republican presidents, the American political system is a Leviathan. It moves ponderously with its own inexorable momentum, and without much regard for electoral outcomes. It is, furthermore, paradoxically impossible to know at the time how much is at stake in any presidential election. This is so, firstly, because of the degree to which the potential future actions of the candidates are clouded in the impenetrable fog of campaign and media spectacle. American voters face the additional difficulty, however, that at the time of the election the public (*and* the candidate) remains unaware of the identity of prospective cabinet members. Yet it may be that the influence wielded by the *appointees*, when combined with the unpredictability of events, will substantially determine the paths taken or abandoned by any particular president. The current Administration, when it comes to matters of foreign policy at least, provides one such case.

If we combine the wisdom of the president and his lieutenant, based on the above quotations, we ought to conclude that there are certain things that we can agree upon. We can agree, for instance, that the past is over: the past is a known known. The future, however, we must agree, is unknown and, as such, it is a known unknown. We cannot agree about any of the unknown unknowns, though, because by definition they escape our present knowledge and, therefore, the possibility of agreement. To *not* know that something is unknown seems to require that we have yet to discover that we do not know. Something that we think we know, that we agree we know, has yet to show itself as something we do not know. We find the unknown unknown, then, in the realm where we wrongly think we are in possession of a known known. That which we have *already* agreed is known may come to reveal to us that in fact our knowledge is false. This is in fact what Rumsfeld is saying, that we should not pretend that we *know* that something has *never* happened if we may only have yet to discover that it has. Known knowns are haunted by the possibility that they may become unknown unknowns. And our agreements, the agreements we have made about what we know, are haunted by the possibility that they were in fact false agreements, agreements made on false premises, prematurely. Perhaps we can never agree that the past is, once and for all, over. The past may return in ways we are yet to know and, as such, not only the future but also the *present* remains a *known* unknown.

In this book we are concerned with the way in which we cannot agree that the past is over. The past is here, in the present, in the form of historical evidence, as ancient pottery, as historical documentation, as unexploded munitions, as the genetic record we receive at conception that reaches back not only to our parents but to our mutual amoebic ancestry. Whether it is encoded DNA or the Rosetta Stone, this evidence works as signs of the past to be read, as knowledge we can uncover. That the past remains is therefore a known known. The past is *present* in the form of historical evidence, but these signs are of that which is now *absent*, of the civilization that has vanished or the reptile that has been evolutionarily superseded. That the signs are *historical* evidence signals first of all that the past is present *only* in the form of signs.

But the past remains also in signs that are yet to be read, that may never be read. Perhaps there are signs that are utterly unreadable. Rather than being simply over, the past may still be playing itself out, in historical effects or rhythms that may take years, centuries or millennia. That we may not have come to know these influences or these rhythms does not constitute evidence that unknown unknowns are not, at this moment, at work. Perhaps a remark of Socrates recorded by Plato, or a remark that Plato *failed* to record, continues to leave its mark on the direction of events in unimaginable ways. The panic and fear produced by the bubonic plague in past centuries may have left its mark in the way in which following generations relate to the possibility of illness, without any awareness of this connection. The transformation of the home that came with the invention of the video recorder and the internet – and the subsequent explosive proliferation of pornography – may have transformed human relations in ways we only think we understand. We ourselves, then, become the signs to be read. "We are a sign that is not read," as the poet Friedrich Hölderlin put it. Agreement about the true character of the present cannot begin with the presupposition that the past is over. The past may be yet to come.

Our current situation, the present, is haunted by the past, in ways both known and as yet unknown. We are haunted by events both remembered and forgotten, recorded and lost, events for which witnesses remain and events the traces of which seem almost utterly to be erased. The calculation of this haunting, of the presence of such ghosts, is perhaps in the end impossible, yet not all ghosts are equally invisible. On the other hand, the haunting of the present by the past is something that is built into the very foundations of politics and society. This is especially visible in the way in which the political institutions of today are *necessarily* haunted by the way in which they began. These two theses are neither particularly difficult nor particularly controversial. The thought that we are haunted, however, produces an almost Freudian resistance, and the structural necessity of this haunting equally means the necessity for forgetting the past. Something may therefore be gained by the contemplation of this haunting and its necessity. The past is never over. The present, however much we may know about it, is constantly confronted by the danger of the revelation that we knew less than we thought. Yet what is dangerous does not always end badly. Recent global events provide one avenue into these questions.

Decisive events

We live in a moment in which there is a widespread *sense* that many of the elements that will determine our future are being played out. Many people have a perception that the immediate present is a period of transition, that a certain path may have ended, and that recent global events suggest a new path may be emerging. If this sense corresponds to something real, the question arises as to when this transitionary phase began. Some would argue that the decisive precipitative event was the fall of the Berlin

Wall or the collapse of the Soviet Union, that is, the end of the Cold War. This was a global political realignment on almost the largest possible scale, with infinitely proliferating consequences. With it, the Remaining Superpower was forced to rethink itself and its place in the world, to rethink the purpose of its military power and the way it was to be deployed, and more generally to reassess what its *ends* are, and the best means for the achievement of those ends.

Others argue that the decisive event took place on 11 September 2001. The end of the Cold War, it could be argued, was merely the end of a fifty-year aberration. Yes, there was the appearance of a "battle of the giants" between, on the one hand, the materialism of communism and the idealism of capitalist freedom. This battle was conducted *as though* it were a struggle about the best and most just way for people to live together under their own rule, politically and economically. It was a sham, however, the argument continues, in the sense firstly that it was not in fact a struggle of ideas but simply a question of military might and global hegemony. It was also a sham, more importantly, because while it served the interests of both "sides" to represent it as a more or less even battle, in reality one side was always utterly dominant. In spite of earth-shattering weaponry on both sides, in retrospect it was always just a matter of awaiting the inevitable crumbling of the weaker side that could never afford the battle in the first place.

What would then have been revealed is that there is only really one "side," and that the planet, in terms of economics and power, is only really one system, rather than two. That the worldwide triumph of capital faced the challenge of another way was merely a phantom of the twentieth century. The Eastern bloc was really just an epi-phenomenon, a hold-out in the face of the overwhelming might of triumphant global capitalism. The process of "globalization" since the fall of communism would then be nothing but the setting into economico-juridical concrete of capitalism's planetary conquest. From the fall of the Berlin Wall, to the replacement of the General Agreement on Trade and Tariffs (GATT) with the World Trade Organization (WTO), nothing was occurring except the formal ratification of what was an obvious reality since the end of World War II: the worldwide empire of the free market.

The hijacking of four planes in September 2001 would not then be the declaration of a new war like the old one. The War on Terror would not be a global struggle between two powers, equivalent to the Cold War ideological battle between communism and capitalism. If this event signaled the commencement of formal hostilities between "Jihad" and "McDonalds," then this is a dispute of a different character. The "enemy" in this case is not a sovereign state or set of states, not an identifiable subject located on the other side of an Iron Curtain, but more like the ghost in the machine, perhaps even the ghost *produced* by the global machine itself. Identification of the enemy is one of the problems for those who would diagnose a new war today. It is the pathological problem, so it seems, of being able to tell the difference between the healthy and the cancerous cells, and of finding a "treatment" that is specific enough to target just those cells that are fatally mutated, without damaging too many of the surrounding healthy and productive organs. In other words, for those who feel that the moment of transition was revealed on 11 September, what matters is that an internal enemy has been brought to the surface, a tumor, perhaps even an inevitable *reaction* produced within the organism itself by its own proper functioning. As such, it is an enemy that is not only difficult to locate and target, but one that, in spite of moments of remission, constantly threatens to return with a vengeance, more powerfully than before, and that it is therefore necessary to strike in a preventive rather than reactive manner.

What is universally referred to now as "terrorism" of course did not begin in September 2001, yet in the aftermath of that event there was a widespread feeling that, for good or ill, things would not be quite the same again. "Terrorism" means a theory and practice of political action that works through the production of mass or public "terror," that is, that operates through the creation of a terrifying *spectacle*. As such, the crashing of two airliners into the Twin Towers, and their subsequent collapse, was obviously a political act of an order of magnitude more successful than any previous terrorist event. The argument of those for whom this was the moment that "changed the world" is that the reverberations from the collapse of the World Trade Center have continued outwards ever since. Inducing widespread fear in the minds of the American (and not only American) public, whatever the motivations and goals of the perpetrators may have been, has determined ever since the course of American foreign relations, and equally decisively influenced domestic relations, for which the creation of a Behemoth ensuring "homeland security" is the clearest example.

Optimism and cynicism

Between these two events – the collapse of the communist states and the collapse of the World Trade Center towers – a document written by Bush II's Deputy Defense Secretary Paul Wolfowitz and rewritten by Bush II's VP Dick Cheney, perhaps proves to be decisive. Wolfowitz is frequently referred to as the "intellect" behind the Rumsfeld group camped at the Pentagon, yet it remains questionable whether and how he is to be identified with the other members of this inner circle. It is the original "Defense Planning Guidance" – written by Wolfowitz during the reign of Bush I in 1992 – which would appear to be most significant. More so, that is, than the Cheney redraft, or the versions of it that have returned as post-11 September White House doctrine, such as the "National Security Strategy." It is necessary to say "appear" in this context, because the original version by Wolfowitz remains classified, and therefore any discussion remains provisional, although extracts from it have been leaked and published. The document is, then, an enigmatic and fragmented talisman, a secret key to the actions of an Administration given to clandestine agendas. What seems clear is that prior to 11 September the Wolfowitz document was too far off the wall even for most Republicans. In the aftermath of 11 September, however, Wolfowitz has come into his own, and his ideas have gained a currency no longer limited to the most hawkish of the Republican hawks, even if these remain his natural allies.

Wolfowitz remains elusive, mostly in the background of White House and Pentagon events. He is, however, an exemplary figure for understanding these events and, more than just the author of the "Defense Planning Guidance," is something like an archetype, through which it is possible to approach the significance of these events. Such constructions carry their own risks, specifically the risk of exaggerating one line of reasoning or explanation. Nevertheless, the vigor with which America is pursuing its goals on foreign shores demands more specific analysis than simply an acknowledgment that "power is operating for the sake of power," or even that "capital is operating for the sake of capital," even if such dogmas still contain their own kernels of truth.

What makes the "Defense Planning Guidance" decisive is the way in which it brings together the close of the Cold War and the opening of the era of the War on Terror. What makes it remarkable is that it does so "pre-emptively," so to speak. The fundamental *observation* that orientates the text is that the United States is by far the greatest power in the world. If this fact was not already completely obvious, the end of the Cold War made it absolutely clear that the power of the United States far exceeds that of any other nation. The fundamental *conclusion* that springs from this observation is that all planning and defense should be guided toward the preservation of this planetary pre-eminence.

> Our first objective is to prevent the re-emergence of a new rival. This is a dominant consideration underlying the new regional defense strategy and requires that we endeavor to prevent any hostile power from dominating a region whose resources would, under consolidated control, be sufficient to generate global power.[1]

To not wield the power America currently has at its disposal would be the worst kind of irresponsible and self-limiting weakness. The "Defense Planning Guidance" is not a work of political philosophy but a government document, and as such it takes as its overriding principle the concept of American "national interest." It could hardly be any other way. Beginning with the observation of American hegemony, then, what guides the Guidance is the question of potential threats to this hegemony. Beyond strategic debate, beyond international obligations and diplomatic conventions, what must be plainly stated, kept in view, and vigorously pursued, is the Higher Purpose. And the Higher Purpose is the furtherance of American interests, or, the furtherance of "America" as such.

What makes the "Defense Planning Guidance" interesting, however, is its peculiar admixture of *optimism* and *cynicism*. This combination positively defines the Wolfowitz doctrine. And, again, it is necessary to speak of appearance, in this case because the strategizing bureaucrat is a figure who always speaks in a kind of code. Even more, the bureaucrat is required to learn a practice of esotericism, to write in such a way that there is a dual message, one for the true readers, the holders of power, and one for the "public." This edict to self-filtrate and self-encrypt operates even where the document in question is not intended to be accessed by that public for, as the leakage of Wolfowitz's "Guidance" itself demonstrates, all contingencies have to be planned for. The continuous redrafting of the original text is less an attempt to rewrite than it is to re-encrypt, to "process" the hard grains of the original in order to render the ideas more digestible to a public less disposed to the harsh realities of *realpolitik*.

And not only for the sake of the American public, but for that broader public known as the international community. If there is such an automatic filtration system in bureaucracy, how much more forcefully it operates when it is a question specifically of "defense," that is, of the relation to actual or potential *enemies*. In the case of the "Defense Planning Guidance," this extends to the consideration of America's official friends and allies (Europe, say) as, now or in the future, America's rivals. Not all enemies are known knowns. The entire logic of "classified" secrets in a democracy has no defensible foundation other than the existence, external or internal, of enemies. Without such a presupposition, it would be absolutely unjustifiable to suppose that public *knowledge* of government activities and government thoughts presented a *danger* to democracy, rather than its precondition.

The Guidance is both cynical and optimistic. What is cynical is the means by which American hegemony is to be protected. Which is to say, so it seems, by any and all means. What is required, it says, is clear-headed and hard-headed assessment of America's actual and potential enemies, whether they threaten with weapons or whether they threaten energy security (that is, unfettered access to oil). American power is currently so great that to *limit* the means for controlling these enemies – to, say, what is legal under international law or sanctioned by the United Nations – is inherently *weak*, and hence unnecessarily threatens the Higher Purpose of American national interest. International law and the United Nations are a global veneer, a global good insofar as their authority applies to *other* nations, but not things about which America needs to be too bothered when greater considerations are in play. And, furthermore, the interest of America obviously means the interests of American capitalism, whether Halliburton or Exxon or any other good corporate citizen. What is most cynical in such strategizing is thus also the automatic convergence of national interest with specific corporate interest. It is tempting to refer the president to the advice he gave to Senator John McCain: "he can't take the high horse and then claim the low road."

What is *optimistic* in the document is the thought that, in pursuit of its self-interest, and in the deployment of these unlimited means, America ought also to encourage the spread of democracy in the rest of the world. The idea that America is a missionary nation spreading the gospel of democracy has a long heritage. Nor is it only an American heritage. The nineteenth-century English colonial adventure, for example, always claimed as one of its goals the export of civilization and – however much profit there was to be had for the East India Company, or in selling opium to the Chinese – it is difficult to deny that this intention was frequently sincere. Nevertheless, it remains the exception for a bureaucrat in the United States Department of Defense, producing an internal global strategic assessment, to argue the need for America to actively produce democracy around the globe. What Wolfowitz seems constantly to express, in this Guidance and in general, is an open zeal for bringing the gift of democracy to those nations of the world unfortunate enough not to share in the benefits of American-style popular rule.

This could perhaps be written off as the encryption referred to above. Is there any more reason to believe that the invasion of Iraq will culminate in "democracy" than there is to believe that the eradication of the Taliban in Afghanistan will end in a functioning modern parliamentary system of governance? Given that France supplied Iraq with its "nuclear" ingredients, Germany supplied its "chemical" ingredients, and America supplied its "biological" ingredients, is it not reasonable to see the entire debate about weapons inspections versus regime change as essentially a wholesalers' dispute? Is it not obvious that, whatever the specifics of the motivations for invasion, events would not quite have transpired as they have if Iraq was not sitting on an ocean of oil? Or, alternatively, is not American foreign policy itself more or less determined by domestic electoral strategy, by party politics and in terms of domestic political advantage? Nevertheless, and in spite of the continuous temptation to view such Wolfowitzian optimism through the lens of one's own cynicism, what distinguishes Wolfowitz from his colleagues in the Administration, and what he may in fact be at some level transmitting *to* these colleagues, is not only his fervor for "regime change." What he also constantly reiterates is the belief that by invading Iraq America is exporting a fundamental good, democracy, to other peoples.

This apparent faith in and commitment to democracy by Wolfowitz is why the "Defense Planning Guidance" is simultaneously cynical and optimistic, Machiavellian yet orientated by democratic faith, following the low road and getting on the high horse. There is almost a kind of naïveté in writing defense strategy in such a baldly Hobbesian and yet simultaneously idealistic tone. Even where Wolfowitz is granting license to American military adventures outside international law, even where he is justifying not only "preemption" but acts of military *prevention*, the very act of daring to commit such thoughts to paper reveals a kind of simple belief that democracy requires truthful speech.

Vice President Cheney was already telling Deputy Defense Secretary Wolfowitz to quieten down about Iraq in early October 2002. This mild muzzling reveals that Wolfowitz, in pushing this agenda, was guilty of being rather impolitic, of speaking too openly about the desire to invade another sovereign nation. Furthermore, however much Wolfowitz may have believed that Iraqi weapons were a threat to the United States, he was, of all prominent members of the Administration, always the one most likely to point to *other* reasons for the invasion. These other reasons – essentially that invading Iraq was on the whole a good thing in itself, *both* for America and for Iraq – could not be used to convince either the public or other nations that the invasion was justified or legal, but there is the appearance at least that for Wolfowitz these were the real reasons.

Of course, there is every reason to see another layer of cynicism over and beyond this apparent optimism. To what extent, for instance, will this commitment to exporting democracy be tempered or abandoned as a result of the obstacles encountered within those countries to which it is being exported? Where the fundamental justification for this democratic imperialism is the national interest, it is always sacrificeable on the very same altar. Nevertheless, this commitment to the national interest comes across in Wolfowitz, insofar as it is possible to tell, as the cynicism of absolute sovereignty. In other words, for America there is no god, nothing more powerful, and as such, what strategic thinking demands is a form of reason capable of thinking this sovereign status. When all divinities are eliminated, when there is no longer anything certain beyond oneself, the inevitable tendency is to think *oneself* divine, that is, sovereign.

The historical transition from theological to secular thinking was largely a matter of the deification of humanity. So too the recognition or the faith that America is beholden to nobody and master of its own destiny inevitably results in a deification of America and American purposes. American foreign policy has been criticized in recent times for continually rebuking others for failing to heed the "rules" it only haphazardly applies to itself. America justifies war for the purposes of removing weapons of mass destruction while holding the largest nuclear arsenal in the world. America ignores the will of the Security Council on the grounds that another nation has ignored the will of the Security Council. America threatens consequences for those who contravene the Geneva Convention, while resolutely insisting that this convention does not apply to those prisoners it holds in Guantanamo Bay. And the "Defense Planning Guidance" argues on the one hand that the United States should aim to "promote increasing respect for international law, limit international violence, and encourage the spread of democratic forms of government." Yet the very same document does not hesitate also to state that what is most important is "the sense that the world order is ultimately backed by the US," and that, therefore, "the United States should be postured to act independently when collective action cannot be orchestrated." Is not the hypocrisy transparent?

Such criticisms fail to grasp, however, that it is not a contradiction so much as a "logic of the exception." The king, traditionally, is not bound by the rules of parliament, the existence of which is itself only a matter of royal decree, to be revoked at the whim of the monarch. It is an error to imagine that the United Nations is a global parliament of which the United States is one member among others. Rather, the United Nations resembles the parliaments of earlier days, with strictly delimited powers. The laws it promulgates, however much they must be enforced against the global citizenry, may always be ignored or over-ruled by the sovereign power that decrees the very possibility of such a parliament and its laws. This is only slightly exaggerated.

What is important for the sovereign power is, as the "Defense Planning Guidance" argues, respect for the law from all of its citizens, and the sense that what lies behind and backs that order is the sovereign power itself. But in spite of demanding respect for the law, the sovereign always reserves the prerogative to act outside this law in exceptional circumstances, just as it reserves the right to decide *when* circumstances *are* exceptional. That is why the president *chose* to turn to the United Nations Security Council to receive its endorsement for an invasion of Iraq, just as he could then *choose* to ignore that body when it failed to provide the endorsement he wanted. As the exceptional power, as the guarantor of the sense of world order, American action is assured of its propriety. America is king.

Wolfowitz, Bloom, Strauss

By what logic would such thinking grasp itself as a commitment to democracy, either American or exported? Perhaps in the cynical-optimistic sense invoked by Churchill in 1947, when he famously stated in parliament:

> No one pretends that democracy is perfect or all-wise. Indeed, it has been said that democracy is the worst form of Government except all those other forms that have been tried from time to time.[2]

This is conservatism in the truest sense, committed to a democratic future on the basis of all the tyrannical crimes of history. Democracy is born, from Greek times onward, out of tyrannicide, the memory of which then becomes the ever-present justification of the current democratic system. It should not be forgotten that Wolfowitz is descended from that conservative intellectual tradition that runs from Leo Strauss to Allan Bloom. Bloom, who died in 1992, is most famous or infamous for his assault on the modern American university and the pernicious effects of "the sixties," the massive bestseller *The Closing of the American Mind*. He is also responsible for probably the best translation/commentary on Plato's *Republic* available in the English language. He is something like the American version, at the *end* of the twentieth century, of what Oswald Spengler was for Germany at its beginning. Both men were the intellectual heroes of the right wing of their day. *The Closing of the American Mind* and *The Decline of the West* both sold in enormous numbers, and both did so by arguing, via a mass of historical and philosophical detail – the specifics of which were attacked by their critics – that contemporary society is suffering under the weight of intellectual and cultural decadence.

Saul Bellow recently published a *roman à clef* on Allan Bloom, *Ravelstein*, in which there is a very minor character widely understood to represent Paul Wolfowitz. If we can be forgiven for translating from fiction to reality, then in Bloom's view Wolfowitz is distinguished among his students by the degree of his grasp of "Great Politics."[3] Wolfowitz can be seen, perhaps, as belonging within that strange branch of quasi-politico-philosophical thought characterized by Francis Fukuyama's thesis of "the end of history."[4] Wolfowitz is apparently a friend of Fukuyama, who was himself another member of Bloom's circle of students. Fukuyama portrays his thought as a modern Hegelianism. It sees America as *finally* triumphant, and triumphant because it deserves to triumph, because it is the triumph of reason. And this must be understood with all of the ambivalence toward reason that characterizes this tradition (for Bloom, for instance, in the age of reason the purpose of the university is to protect reason from itself).

If this is an American intellectual heritage, it is also a Jewish one or, more accurately, a heritage that begins by taking note of the fact of the Jewish extermination by the Nazis. Leo Strauss is the father of a considerable intellectual heritage in American political thought. He founds his thinking in a profound skepticism about political possibilities, and the memory of the extermination seems ever present as an implicit rebuttal to political hope. This is the case, even though his thought is equally founded in true appreciation of the genius of the political philosophical tradition. For Strauss the liberalism of capitalist democracy could only ever be a weak protection against the capacity of man to inflict mass murder against "a people." Yet the risks and dangers of "stronger" approaches to political organization pushed him toward the necessity and urgency of *defending* democracy, which too easily weakens *itself* through misplaced faith in its own ideals. Consider the following sentence concerning the role of Nietzsche in the formation of the Third Reich: "He thus prepared a regime which, as long as it lasted, made discredited democracy look again like the golden age." This is a more intense and pessimistic revision of the Churchillian defense of democracy. Understanding Paul Wolfowitz may be a matter of putting this disjointed set of fragments together.

In speaking of a line of descent from Strauss to Bloom to Wolfowitz, it is first necessary to rule out any cabal or conspiracy to dominate American political life, either for its own sake or "on behalf of" Israel. The temptation to this strain of global conspiracy anti-semitism can all too often still be observed, if it is not in fact on the increase. Such anti-semitism is, furthermore, just as common on the left as it is on the right, where Larouchian diatribes represent only its most visible form. Such anti-semitism, regardless of its political orientation, always involves a bristling about the fact that such permanent "outsiders" are able to operate in the very centre of "our" democracy. It is always a matter of infiltration, an *internal* threat, an invisible foreign presence occupying the heart of politics.

This tone is audible in the argument one hears that Wolfowitz's *real* motivation is to distract attention from his true concern, which is Israel and its ability to resist international pressure in relation to the Palestinians (is he not an associate of Netanyahu?). Wolfowitz, and those "like him," this argument goes, are the shadowy presence of a foreign element that has crossed the border, reached the seat of power, and distorted the properly democratic character of American political institutions. It may indeed be possible to trace nexuses of influence between Israeli political and military élites and the Wolfowitzes of Washington. Nevertheless, this does not mean that Strauss or Bloom have "infiltrated" American foreign policy by introducing their agent, Wolfowitz.

If what motivates somebody like Wolfowitz in the eyes of Bloom (via *Ravelstein*) is a grasp of Great Politics, then this must be understood correctly. "Great Politics" does not refer merely to a Machiavellian understanding of politics as the Great Game. The Cold War always had a sense of gamesmanship, as can be seen in the way it was represented in thriller fiction, where the Soviet spies, if not exactly gentlemen, are nevertheless as worldly wise and sophisticated as their British or American counterparts – terrorists are rarely portrayed in such a fashion. Beyond gamesmanship, "Great Politics" means grasping the political at the highest level, playing with the greatest stakes, shaping the world and thinking on a globally strategic level. More than this, it means playing the game with the greatest stakes because *what* is at stake is of the utmost seriousness, that is, the possibility of the return of the absolute worst. "Great Politics" means a Machiavellianism informed by, or rather *haunted* by, the extermination undertaken in Nazi Germany. The quasi-idealist yet utterly "realist" motivation, then, would be that the hegemony of "American democracy" is, whatever its failings, infinitely preferable to the ghost of that world which enveloped Germany with the fall of the Weimar republic. The commitment to democracy is *founded*, in this conception, not on the validity of democractic theory, but on the reality of this haunting.

Western government after National Socialism – that is, Pax Americana – would then be sovereign democracy, democracy that founds itself on nothing but the *comparative* virtue of its own existence. This would be the positive Nietzschean legacy, a democracy that no longer needed to justify itself on eternal grounds. Strauss concludes:

> For oblivion of eternity, or, in other words, estrangement from man's deepest desires and therewith from the primary issues, is the price which modern man had to pay, from the very beginning, for attempting to be absolutely sovereign, to become the master and owner of nature, to conquer chance.[5]

Sovereignty, proper mastery of oneself, is hereby thought in relation to giving up on immortality. Sovereignty becomes a properly mortal style of thought that starts from the fact of the finality and non-transcendent character of death, and hence of the finitude of life. The mastery involved is not the mastery of reason, but rather "realism" distinguished from "rationalism," the realism of mortal consciousness. Politics, it is being argued, should not be premised on heavenly, that is, immortal, visions but, rather, on the absolute fact of the *certainty* of death, and the equally absolute fact of the *possibility* of mass violent death, of extermination.[6] Yet, as such a mortal, "realistic" form of thought, it remains tied to the mastery and overcoming of nature. But what is "nature" in such a context other than the sign of mortality? And what is the "mastery of nature" other than the empty reign of a technological conception of politics?

It is not a matter of explaining Wolfowitz or American foreign policy on the basis of his association with Allan Bloom, or Bloom's association with Strauss. It is certainly not a matter of demonstrating the effects of Bloomian or Straussian political thought, as though Wolfowitz had "translated" this thought into practice in Washington, as though we could judge the earlier thinker by the later practitioner. Of course, in the passage quoted above, Strauss attempts to make exactly this manouevre in relation to Nietzsche, not directly by stating that National Socialism was "Nietzschean," but indirectly, by arguing that Nietzsche "prepared" the way, laid the ground, for the catastrophe to follow. Perhaps Bloom could be said to have prepared the way for a figure such as Wolfowitz, a figure who apparently (we continue to insist on the need to speak of appearances) represents a variation upon that peculiar and esoteric cynical-optimistic "conservative philosophy" inaugurated in the United States by the immigrant Leo Strauss.

The politics of chance

Politics, democracy, as the conquering of risk: this suggests a strange relation between America and chance. On the one hand, the sovereignty of America, the absolute certainty of American hegemony, and the certainty that this hegemony is a global good, represents a belief in the elimination of chance. Since 11 September George W Bush has spoken of little other than certainties – the certainty of victory, the certainty of the morality of American action, the certainty of utter defeat for the enemy.[7] The assertion of the absolute sovereignty of America is something like a tonic offered to the American public to counter the *un*certain feelings provoked by the "first attack on American soil." On the other hand, the religion of America, that is, capitalism, is itself properly a religion *of* chance, that places its faith explicitly in the gods of chance and speculation. The proper capitalist is the master of what Paul Auster calls "the music of chance," the harmony of the spheres, the theological aspect of which sees the cogs of the capitalist machinery as identical with the rhythmical yet chance-driven movements of the universal celestial bodies.

The conquest *of* chance proves to be the same thing as conquest *by* chance. Such a thought draws Wolfowitz's "Great Politics" to the penultimate chapter of *The Prince*, according to which the great Prince is not the one who imagines he can eliminate chance, *fortuna*, but the one for whom the crucial realization is the necessity of accepting, finitely, that absolute control is impossible. For the Prince, there can be no final certainty but, on the other hand, giving up sight of final ends opens the possibility of proper circumspection about the present and the future. Loosening one's grip on the final destination makes it possible to play *with fortuna*, to gamble wisely, to make one's own luck. Fortune is a river that constantly threatens to overwhelm us, and we cannot simply swim toward our goal on the other shore, but must calculate our direction in relation to a powerful current against which we are relatively impotent. Nevertheless, Machiavelli concludes, it is a calculation about which it is better to be impetuous rather than overly cautious, for "*Fortuna* is a woman," who requires a struggle and prefers audacity.

It seems, therefore, as though Machiavelli sides with the audacity of the Defense Department over the pragmatism of the State Department, with the shaping of the world over the building of Fortress America. Paul Wolfowitz may then be something like the ill-fated Dr Mesmer in Lars von Trier's movie, *Epidemic*.[8] Faced with the onset of an epidemic, the government resigns, each ministerial portfolio to be filled by a doctor, that is, by technocratic experts, whose first decision is to turn the city into a fortress to control contamination. Dr Mesmer, however, is an "idealist," who cannot accept abdicating his therapeutic role in favor of merely pragmatic containment. Consequently he leaves the fortress to administer to the affected in outlying areas, even though he has no effective treatment. What

Mesmer fails to realize, however, is that he himself is infected. In spite of or in fact because of his idealism, Mesmer is instrumental in the further spread of the epidemic. In the end, he is forced to acknowledge that his idealism, for all the worthiness of the ideals, was in fact just as dangerous as the pragmatism of the fortress-builders.

Wolfowitz recognizes along with the pragmatists the illness of the outside world. The pragmatists understand the disease as the growth and prevalence of terrorism, but for Wolfowitz it is more profoundly the epidemic of injustice, of oppression, and of dictatorship. Contrary to the experts in containment – pragmatists and isolationists – Wolfowitz argues that true protection from contamination demands engagement with the infected areas, and administration of proper treatment. The treatment in this case is the removal of the "bad regime" and its replacement by "good government": openness, freedom, democracy. The risk he faces is that, in advocating forceful if not indeed violently "Machiavellian" means for the elimination of the disease, he may in fact be the instrument of its transmission. Wolfowitz's idealism and optimism risks ending in the acknowledgment of its own pathological condition.

But for Machiavelli it is not a given but a matter of calculation whether the Prince should protect himself from his subjects by building a fortress. It is a matter of relative dangers, of whether there is more to fear from those within or those outside the borders of the principality. A fortress is a barrier for the Prince against the hatred of his citizenry. As such, however, a fortress also limits communication with and control over these citizens, entailing risk in the face of external threats. Machiavelli is as usual concise and to the point:

> So we see that fortresses are useful or not depending on circumstances; and if they are beneficial in one direction, they are harmful in another. It can be put like this: the prince who is more afraid of his own people than of foreign interference should build fortresses; but the prince who fears foreign interference more than his own people should forget about them.[9]

This account of walls and dangers is generally applicable. In the argument we are constructing here the walls of the fortress are the walls of America, and the borders of the principality are the planet itself. The calculation is not whether the American people represent a danger. Rather, what is to be calculated is the degree of threat from beyond the American fortress, from which direction it comes, and by what means it is to be contained.

We have suggested that Machiavelli's fondness for audacity over caution puts him in the Rumsfeld and Wolfowitz camp, rather than that of Colin Powell's pragmatic "realism" in relation to the exercise of military muscle. But it is also possible to see the matter in a precisely opposite way. The indifference to diplomacy, to international law, to "world opinion," that characterizes the Pentagon hawks, might in fact be grasped as the real fortress-building. This version of the analogy with Machiavelli requires thinking of the "international community" as the global "citizens" within the American principality. The withdrawal of contact, the gradual closing of proper and open channels of communication with these world citizens, is the act of calculating that the "family of nations" represent the greatest threat, compared to something that lies beyond these "legitimate" nations. Because the members of the Security Council et al are the real threat, the threat of the emergence of a *rival*, walls to protect America from them must be maintained. That is, a genuine coalition or consensus in relation to Iraq may be sacrificed. Unilateral action is preferable to granting influence to "Old Europe" or new China, even if we cannot openly speak of them (yet) as the enemy.

By contrast, to remain "engaged" with the world, to take seriously the necessity of diplomacy and the recognition of international legality, to speak of the need for friends and partners, would be the calculation that the threat from "outside," from rogue nations, global terrorists etc., is the real danger. It is the calculation that the threat is so great that it is better to maintain good relations with the neighbors, just in case it turns out that their assistance is required. Maintaining contact and communication is the necessary price to pay to control this danger, even at the price of ceding some autonomy, that is, some sovereignty, when it comes to countering those dangers that come to us from outside. According to this thought, the policy of Fortress America fails to take the external danger seriously enough, and overstates the consequences of maintaining the friendship of the international community, America's subjects.

The question to be addressed to the Pentagon hawks is this: if the danger from outside, from terrorism, is as serious as *they contend*, can America afford to build this kind of fortress between itself and the international community? Or is the logic of the "Defense Planning Guidance" operating within the Administration dictating that the real concern is to prevent the emergence of a rival power? If so, is this not to admit that, whatever the public posturing about terrorism and rogue nations, the real consideration orienting foreign policy is America's pre-eminence in relation to Europe, China, etc.? Iraq and al Qaeda may be the *ostensible* targets of American foreign policy, and Iraq may represent a possible rival at the level of energy security, but at the clandestine level, the esoteric truth determining policy options sees the real danger elsewhere.

Do these policy-makers really see terrorism and rogue states as the danger, or is another, longer term threat claiming their attention? Undoubtedly the thought of weapons of mass destruction in the hands of psychopathic ideologues is frightening, but one does not need to go to Iraq to find WMD, and psychopaths lurk in every government. It seems likely that both agendas operate – the concern with terrorism, with the Middle East "problem," etc., and the concern with the long term fate of America and its status as global sovereign, global emperor. This perhaps accounts for the ambivalence and uncertainty the Administration has demonstrated in relation to its own initial preparedness to stand alone against Iraq. For those like Paul Wolfowitz, the key to both these policy directions is the thought that American security is paramount, not because America is pure, but as a bulwark against the return of the absolute worst.

To what extent is the enemy real, to what extent a phantasm, or a ghost that haunts the minds of American policy-makers? Is there an identifiable and fatally dangerous epidemic, and is there the knowledge and the means for any effective treatment? Whenever an enemy is declared, the comparison to Hitler is inevitably made. This is of course largely a matter of public relations, but that just begs the question – from where comes the lasting force of such a public relations manoeuvre? To take a ghost – the ghost of the worst – as the enemy, would mean to risk becoming possessed, to risk being determined by and coming to share the character of that which continues to haunt oneself as the enemy-to-come. But this is not to say that there is no such thing as ghosts, nor that they cannot indeed return.

Paul Wolfowitz, playing Machiavelli to Prince Bush *il Magnifico*, has staked his political future on his audacious or grandiose Iraq policy, but what is at stake obviously exceeds the question of whether this policy will prove personally fortunate for its author. What is most questionable or hubristic in the current direction of American foreign policy is the degree to which its executors seem to believe that chance is a factor that can be overcome or, at least, bridled. The risk, in cynically-optimistically playing politically with the greatest stakes, is that the original tragic, haunted sense of politics that gave the initial impetus to what is being undertaken – that is, the remembrance of the possibility of the worst – will be entirely forgotten in the playing out of the triumphalist game of power.

Chapter 2

Strangers in a Familiar Land

Freedom of conscience requires secular government. But what makes secular law legitimate? That question is the starting point of Western political philosophy, and is now mired in academic controversy. But, to cut an interminable story indecently short, the consensus among modern thinkers is that the law is made legitimate by the consent of those who must obey it. This consent is shown in two ways: by a real or implied "social contract," whereby each person agrees with every other to the principles of government; and by a political process through which each person participates in the making and enacting of the law. The right and duty of participation is what we mean, or ought to mean, by "citizenship," and the distinction between political and religious communities can be summed up in the view that the first are composed of citizens, the second of subjects.

Roger Scruton[1]

The past remains. The mixture of cynicism and optimism that seems to define the thought of key strategists or policy-makers in the current United States administration, it was suggested, is evidence of a haunted relation to the past. The heritage of thought that leads from Leo Strauss to Allan Bloom to Paul Wolfowitz indicates a way of thinking that remains in many ways a reaction to the devastating events of the National Socialist period in Germany. But this haunted relation to the past is not confined to the minds of government strategists. Rather, there is a "structural" and ineradicably "destructuring" presence of the past at the level of political foundation. In this chapter we will examine the meaning of this claim.

This chapter was begun as the government of one sovereign state succumbed to the military might of another. It is a climactic moment in a long process, one important preliminary element of which was an intense effort by the invading forces to convince their domestic audience of the necessity of the act. The means of persuasion was the construction of a rhetoric comprising three essential parts: (1) that the state to be invaded not only possesses military strength, but possesses in its arsenal weapons that are more "horrific" or "dangerous" than the conventional weapons in the arsenal of every state, *that is, it possesses weapons of mass destruction*; (2) that the state, although sovereign, is illegitimate, less for internal reasons or because of its origins than because of its wayward, erratic, and unpredictable foreign policy, because the state cannot be trusted to behave the way proper states such as ourselves can be counted to do, *that is, it is a rogue state*; (3) that beyond the possession of these weapons, and beyond its own roguish ways, the state may be the catalyst for the delivery and use of weapons of mass destruction on faraway foreign shores, and that it may be this catalyst through its association with non-state actors of evil intent, *that is, it has an association with terrorists*.

The rhetoric functions crudely, at an almost fantastical level, but effectively. What is more it can be applied at will to a string of nations. Each of the three elements is necessary for the painting of the overall scene, and none of them without the others is sufficient to justify military intervention. "Justify," here, means to the domestic population whose citizens will constitute the soldiers and pilots at risk during any intervention. The possession of destructive weapons is an insufficient trigger, as the most destructive weapons are almost all in the hands of America and those nations against which there is no intention to act whatsoever (if for no other reason than that they *do* possess these weapons). That a state may be roguish is insufficient for a claim for the need of "pre-emptive self-defense," unless that roguishness is *directly* threatening. All the pieces must be put together.

The argument, then, is as follows: a state is roguish and therefore capable of anything; it possesses weapons which threaten horrifying consequences if unleashed; and it has the *means* for the delivery of these weapons to domestic shores, that is, by placing them in the hands of terrorists who, as we know since 11 September 2001, can achieve any goal. This triumvirate of claims formed an incantation that was recited as a daily prayer by the representatives of the "coalition of the willing" in the months leading up to the invasion of Iraq. Untold effort was expended seeking or manufacturing evidence for these claims, establishing the apparent need for their final verification in the aftermath of invasion.

Yet this aftermath has served to make clear that this threefold rhetoric has reached the end of its usefulness for the invaders (at least in relation to Iraq). What is more, that the invasion is a *fait accompli* means that the existence of these weapons is more or less irrelevant to the direction of future events, however much they may occupy the media. There is embarrassment that no proof of chemical or biological weapons has been discovered, and there will be inquiries and investigations. A war was based on this claim, yet this embarrassment is more or less easily shrugged off, and intelligence, that is, bureaucracy, can easily swallow the blame for false claims. What matters now, it is glibly pointed out, is not the past but the future of Iraq.

Henceforth if the legitimacy of the invasion is questioned, the overwhelming argument is that what took place was a welcome liberation. The ends justified the means. No further justification is necessary, and no further evidence is important. The consent of the "beneficiaries" ensures legitimacy. Any further debate about the sincerity and validity of the prior insistence on the existence of thousands of barrels of anthrax, on roguish foreign policy, and on association with terrorists, is nothing more than a point of historical debate. To assert that the invading powers justified their invasion on spurious grounds, to assert that they lied to their respective publics in order to build support for the invasion, is to argue against the rationales offered *in the past*, rather than to "deal with the reality" that the invasion has been accomplished.

Of course, the climactic moment is not really the climax, and things can still turn decidedly sour. The extent to which the invaders have been welcomed as liberators is doubtful. So to is the intention and the *capacity* of the invaders to extend to those people liberated the possibility of governing themselves. It is clear that the real purpose of this invasion was to change the regime, even if this could not be explicitly stated during the pre-war publicity blitz. It is far less clear whether the commitment to regime change translates into a commitment to democracy, nor whether all the diligent planning for the aftermath of the invasion ever really came to grips with the scale of the task. If the pre-war rationales were merely lies and machinations, the more important question is whether it can be legitimate for one state to remove the government of another state and engineer its replacement.

Democratic imperialism

Can it be legitimate for one sovereign nation to invade another sovereign nation on the basis that it intends to *give* or *bring* democracy to the people it is invading? The argument that it is legitimate to export democracy begins, more or less, with the "Defense Planning Guidance" of Paul Wolfowitz. What is truly odd about this thought is the possibility that it is based in some kind of sincere faith in the *necessity* of exporting democracy. The world has never previously seen, we would argue, such an apparently theological commitment to "democratic imperialism." There is, of course, every reason in the world to remain cynical about such a venture, about such foreign policy adventurism, and first of all about whether that is really what is taking place. Nevertheless, papers have already begun to appear in political science journals arguing for the proper conditions and the right way to go about spreading democracy imperially. Whether it is finally to be understood as something real or illusory, there is at least the simulacrum of an event here. Yet the question remains: is democracy exportable?

If the case is accepted that democracy is exportable and it is legitimate to do so, then the pretext may have been established for many a future act of "pre-emption." In the Cold War era invasion was justified not on the grounds of bringing democracy, but rather on the somewhat limited grounds of preventing the creep of communism. From Korea and Vietnam to Nicaragua and the fight against the Soviet occupation of Afghanistan, there was only the veneer of a concern for democracy, and a far greater concern for the relative distribution of capitalist and non-capitalist states. At the rhetorical level it was always a matter of national security and national interest, however fanciful this rhetoric may in fact have been.

At the *end* of the Cold War, the era of Bill Clinton tends to be associated with military action justified in the name of "humanitarian intervention." The idea of humanitarian intervention is, essentially, non-political, and the public support that can be garnered on the basis of this idea is fundamentally fragile. Thousands upon thousands of people suffer and die, are tortured or murdered, lead miserable and short lives due to poverty, disease and oppression, all over the globe, every single day. The collective citizenry of the first world, for instance, is fully able to tolerate the deaths of millions due to AIDS, so long as the vast majority of these deaths are elsewhere (whereas SARS, on the other hand, threatens among its consequences to bring down major airlines because of the panic it induces among first world populations). It is therefore impossible to rely upon public support for military action on humanitarian grounds in one small corner of the planet, if this action involves any substantial risk to the lives of its own armed forces personnel. The first justification for democracy is the prevention of the suffering of *its own* citizens, and arguments for humanitarian intervention are therefore from the beginning contending *against* the instincts and the duties of democracy itself, wherever such intervention threatens to induce suffering on any of its own people. This was the lesson that emerged from the deaths of American armed forces personnel in Somalia.

In the aftermath of 11 September it may well have been expected that this insularity would intensify, and perhaps it has. The rhetorical effort to justify the invasions of Afghanistan and Iraq, after all, depended upon torturous arguments to establish how they would serve the national interest. Yet it is interesting that accompanying this insularity is another rhetoric, that at the moment remains veiled and only vaguely admitted: that there exists the right to bring democracy to others through the use of force. This argument, whatever threats it contains, is radically political, where humanitarian intervention could never be. There is greater likelihood, we would argue, but no certainty, that domestic populations will support the sacrifices that come with war if the war is for political reasons, for a *cause*, than if it is simply to minimize the suffering of someone somewhere else. More enthusiasm is generated by a crusade than a risky humanitarian rescue. That *we* may suffer in the course of humanitarian action automatically undermines its justification, whereas the crusade absolutely demands preparedness for sacrifice.

Rather than just being a reaction to the fact of suffering, democratic imperialism is the claim that a democratic state has some kind of duty, as a citizen of the world, to act with the goal of ending non-democratic governments everywhere. It is, therefore, inherently an affirmation of our own worth, and a demonstration of the resolution with which we are prepared to share the benefits of that worth. Political institutions become once again not merely an impersonal and technological arrangement for our mutual protection, but rather a properly political form of life, involving each one of its citizens at the core of their being, committed to the political virtues and demanding sacrifice for the greater cause of political life. How much less effective would be the chant of the protesters if they really were forced to change from "No blood for oil" to "No blood for democracy"?

This Aristotelian presentation of current events is certainly grandiose, but the possibility that reason and rhetoric are today being transformed in this direction demands our consideration. The feeling that there is something threatening about this comes mostly from observing *who* constitute the vanguard of this democratic imperialism. Is it really possible to believe that George W Bush and Donald Rumsfeld act from the motive of saving the world for democracy? Is not the manner of Bush's "election" sufficient to suggest that he prefers to save himself *from* democracy? The suspicion about democratic imperialism, however, also arises from a more fundamental question. How can democracy, the self-governance of those within the borders of a state, *possibly* be delivered to the people of a state *from outside*? Is not the giving of democracy from outside necessarily the imposition of a system, rather than the act *of* a people to decide to follow a certain, "democratic" path? Is not democracy something that only "we" can give to ourselves?

The dangerous, threatening, and indeed hubristic character of the argument that democracy is exportable is unquestionable. Armed with the "morality" of bringing democratic enlightenment to the unenlightened and the subjugated, the powerful may be able to shape the world, *not* in its image, but according to its needs or wishes. It is this possibility that most immediately and concretely makes the second Gulf War a potentially decisive historical event. This danger, and this threat, it may be added, are not only for the receivers, but also for those who are doing the bringing.

Nevertheless, the apparent obviousness of the contradiction involved in "bringing democracy in from the outside" is itself questionable. What it presupposes, first of all, is the distinction between inside and outside, that is, a border. The world has seen the construction of a border between those countries that understand themselves as democratic, and the rest. But for each one of those "democratic" nations, the concept of the border is fundamental. It is at the heart of the very idea of democracy, both for those who wish to export it, and for those who see this as *a priori* impossible. As a way into such questions, one recent text that constructs such borders and theorizes them will serve as an example: Roger Scruton's *The West and the Rest: Globalization and the Terrorist Threat.*

Religion and politics

In the last couple of years a publishing industry has emerged preoccupied with the difference between "us" and "them," where the latter is defined as those who, if not all bad are nevertheless, and unlike "us," the breeders of terrorists. The philosopher Roger Scruton has been as industrious as the best of them. His attempt to locate the contours of the fault line between the West and the rest, between the globalizers and the terrorizers, leads him to the recognition that what must be explained is less "their evil" than "our virtue." To this end, Scruton retraces within a few pages some of the key themes in the history of Western political thought. The economy of this recapitulation, combined with the intent of the author, make this work of popular political philosophy particularly useful for our own overly economical reflection on the same themes. The thrust of his overall argument about the difference between the West and the rest will not be pursued closely here. Rather, an examination of the beginnings and presuppositions of his account of the West will illuminate some of the characteristic ways and means by which "we" grasp ourselves as *properly* political, that is, democratic.

Scruton begins his account with "religion," and with the origin of the word in "*ligere*," "to bind." He grasps this etymology in a way that is immediately political, understanding the "bond" in question to be that of the community with itself, rather than, say, the bond of mortals to the divine. From the very beginning, therefore, for Scruton religion is not only an article of faith. More than simply a matter of "social function," religion is for Scruton the very question of the political, the question of what is the proper way for man to be bonded to man. The difference between the West and the rest that he outlines is essentially a matter of different kinds of binding. Scruton is peculiarly bound to religion, and the manner in which he pursues the question oscillates in a strange way in relation to the religious. His argument plays itself out in the elastic back and forth of his account of the political truth and significance of the religious bind.

In short, for Scruton religion is political, yet the religious is at the same time to be rigorously differentiated *from* the political. This can already be seen in the way in which he cites his very first example, Sophocles' *Antigone*. Scruton is not the first to see the tragedy as the prototypical political document, nor the first to see it as the staging of the conflict between religion and politics. Creon, the tyrant who upholds his civic right to deny burial to Antigone's brother on the grounds of treason, is the embodiment of the political. Antigone, who insists on her brother's right to a proper burial, embodies the religious. Such a reading of the tragedy finds its most elaborate formulation in Hegel. Yet this reading is certainly open to challenge, first of all for presuming that the political and religious orders are at the time of Sophocles' writing differentiated from one another. It is just as possible to read the tragedy, as Jean-Pierre Vernant does, as a conflict *within* the religious, between two conceptions of the religious, between the religious as centred on the city (the public) and the religious as centred on the home (the private).[2] Or, put another way, as the conflict between one conception of law and another, a staging at a primordial moment in Greek law of an antagonism within it.

For Scruton, however, the point is not essential, because if *Antigone* is the first example, it is nevertheless only with the intervention of two phenomena that the political and the religious really emerge historically. First, Roman law introduces the "universalism" necessary for the governance of faraway colonies. Second, the Christianity founded by Paul for the first time insists on the need to bring faith to all of humanity, and hence inaugurates a notion of "universal citizenship." Only after these events does the idea of a sovereign and universal *law* really make itself known. Law then – proper, self-standing law – commences with this dual historical phenomenon of a universal jurisdiction and a universal church.

Yet, despite this dual origin, Scruton's point is to *contrast* the political and the religious, in order to attribute the former to the West and the latter to the rest. What makes secular law legitimate according to Scruton is *consent* (the "social contract") and participation (the political process). This differentiates the "citizens" of "political communities" from the "subjects" of "religious communities." The bind in the latter case is still of each subject to God. The dual origin of secular law, which is both a political *and* a religious origin, is thereby used by Scruton for the *differentiation* of the properly political from the non-political religious community. The political is defined in relation to the religious in a way that does not merely set them apart from each other as antitheses. Rather, the political is involved from the beginning and in an intimate way with the religious. Yet the apparent intention of Scruton's argument is to separate two kinds of community, two ways of binding people to one another, on the basis of a distinction between political binding and religious binding.

Territorial jurisdiction

What is common to Roman law and Pauline faith, then, is the inauguration of "universalism." They embody the dual origin of the thought that law, whether religious or political, exceeds its previously local, finite character. Yet when Scruton comes to examine secular law and its virtues more specifically, that is, when he examines the order of the properly political community, this universalism is strangely deflected by a preoccupation with the specific. The phrase to which Scruton continually resorts when accounting for the virtue of secular (political) law, is "territorial jurisdiction."

Again and again Scruton sings the praises of territorial jurisdiction, reciting it as a kind of prayer or anthem, whether religious or national. This notion, the thought of "universal" law bounded to a specific territory, will be Scruton's exit from the religious and his substitute for it. On page 24 he argues that where law is defined over territory, it becomes "detached from the demands of religion and [is] reconstrued as an abstract system of rights and duties." The social contract is described on page 35 as "a kind of theological abstraction from the experience of territorial jurisdiction." On page 55 Scruton states that the crucial feature of the republican constitution is not democracy, but representation, "and this in turn requires a territorial jurisdiction, along with the loyalties that feed it." On page 66 one of the virtues of the West is accounted for as follows: "Religious toleration is the norm in Western societies precisely because they are founded on a territorial jurisdiction that regards sovereignty rather than divinity as the source of law." That this virtue distinguishes the West from the rest is made clear on page 125: "By contrast, Islam, which has been until recently remote from the Western world and without the ability to project its own message, is founded on an ideal of godliness which is entirely global in its significance, and which regards territorial jurisdiction and national loyalty as compromises with no intrinsic legitimacy of their own." Finally, on page 149, it becomes clear that if universalism is the thought that underlies secular law at its origin, this nevertheless is in no way inconsistent for Scruton with a strongly enforced policy of border protection to prevent the dilution of the proper character of the Western territories:

> The political and economic advantages that lead people to seek asylum in the West are the result of territorial jurisdiction. Yet territorial jurisdictions can survive only if borders are controlled. Transnational legislation, acting together with the culture of repudiation, is therefore rapidly undermining the conditions that make Western freedom durable. The effect of this on the politics of France and Holland is now evident to everyone. And when we find among the "asylum seekers" the vast majority of those Islamist cells that have grown

up in London, Paris, and Hamburg, we begin to recognize just how much the political culture of the West is bent on a path of self-destruction.[3]

It is not exaggerating to argue that what Scruton intends most to defend is this notion of territorial jurisdiction, nor to say that for Scruton this defense is more important than mounting a defense of even democracy. For Scruton it is territorial jurisdiction that explains the virtues to be found in the West, the virtues of "law-abidingness, sacrifice in war, and public spirit in peacetime," virtues that can be found in Muslim society only in a secondary way as deriving from the duties owed to God.[4] It is *as* societies founded on territorial jurisdiction, on national law, that the societies of the West embody political, as opposed to religious, virtue.

Law and territory. What makes it so important for Scruton to bring these together when defining the order of the properly political? The answer lies in what opened his book, in the thought of the "bind," the bind that from the beginning entwines the political and the religious. Scruton is responding to his fear that within this bind lies the danger, the threat of society binding itself too tightly to the religious bond. He is responding at the same time to his fear that without binding – where the bond between people is allowed to unbind itself – community itself will evaporate and politics will become impossible.

For Scruton, the bind is both the danger and the promise. Religious fundamentalism, and law based on divine commandment, are those features of a society committed too strongly to the bind between the mortal and the divine. Yet without binding Scruton cannot see that secular law could ever maintain its legitimacy. Thus, he argues, without "membership" the social contract crumbles. Indeed, in the face of globalization and international lawmaking, it is this very legitimacy of national law that Scruton feels is threatened. "Territorial jurisdiction" is the *deus ex machina* that Scruton thinks will find him a way out of this bind.

That the bond is both the danger and the promise for secular law equally means that the *absence* of binding is both the danger and the promise. Thus Scruton is just as ambivalent about the fact that, as he puts it, "modern democracy is perforce a society of strangers."[5]

The sense and the reality that in today's society we are strangers to one another is the very basis for the form of democratic politics "we" have adopted, even if this mutual estrangement also threatens to unravel the political fabric we have so carefully woven for one another. Modern democracy, he is arguing, is a society of bonded strangers.

The difficulties of this proposition, not to say the contradictions, do not entirely escape Scruton's notice. He recognizes that these difficulties afflict the thought of democracy not only in its "modern" guise, but in the very thought of the origins of the "social contract" on which it is founded. Or, rather, he recognizes this problem only to immediately leap to its "solution," of which "territorial jurisdiction" is the main expression. It is very easy to formulate this problem: if the social contract is what founds society then, beyond the question of the "actuality" of this contract, how is it possible for strangers, unbound, to come together in agreement to a contract, without already imagining themselves in some way as bound to one another? Without feeling themselves *already* bound, without already sharing a minimal level of agreement – sharing for instance a common language – how can the conditions of promising that a contract requires possibly be met? Must not the parties to such a contract, which founds law, already recognize, as Scruton puts it, that they possess a common future, that they are *already* bound to one another by some kind of "membership"? In short, does not the social contract presuppose its own existence?

Scruton's formulation of this requirement is as follows: "But if they are in a position to decide on their common future, it is because they already have one," that is, "the social contract requires a relation of membership." The truth of the social contract is that it does not presuppose a group of free individuals, but rather "a first-person plural, in which the burdens of belonging have already been assumed."[6] It presupposes a "we." This "we," being the possibility of the social contract, is necessarily "pre-political," and for Scruton it derives from occupying a "common territory."[7] The strangeness of his version of the social contract is that it is begun by strangers who nonetheless must have "imagined themselves as a community," and who do so by reason of occupying a specific piece of territory. We are strangers in a familiar land. This is the mechanism that permits

Scruton to differentiate secular law from religious law. That the social contract is not founded on a relation to God, but rather on a mutual interrelation based on territory, supposedly abstracts the law it founds from anything religious.

This differentiation between secular and religious law is unpersuasive, because the formula remains identical in both cases. That is, if territory is not God, nevertheless it is that external quality to which each member is bonded, and that *therefore* binds the "members" of a group to one another. A civilized and enlightened man cannot today theorize the bind between members of a group with anything as vulgar as racial identity. Common territory is to some extent the polite version of the same notion. Territory is the substance in common that means that one group of people is ideally suited to distinguishing itself from the rest, and thereby to founding a social contract for itself, a territorial jurisdiction. This, however, was the precise function of God in binding a group together according to religious law. "Territory" succeeds in avoiding the reference to religion only by itself being turned into a theological abstraction.

This fabulous event

The theological aspect of the concept of "territorial jurisdiction" is visible when Scruton insists that the relation between law and a specific territory must not be understood as a mere artifice that inaugurates politics.

> At the same time we must not think of territorial jurisdiction as a merely conventional arrangement, a kind of ongoing and severable agreement of the kind distilled in the social contract theory. It involves, in the normal case, a genuine "we" of membership.[8]

What does the word "genuine" mean in this context? How is it possible to recognize the difference between genuine membership and conventional arrangements? Scruton cites the American Declaration of Independence. Even though the Constitution was adopted without reference to any prior law, thus inaugurating a jurisdiction *ab initio*, a first-person plural was involved, a pre-contractual "we," a genuine membership. That is why the Declaration begins with the words, "We, the people." What is thereby decided, according to Scruton, is not a contract at all, "but a bond of membership."[9]

Whatever truth there is in this account of the meaning of the Declaration, Scruton is too quick to decide on its significance, too quick to resolve the impossibility of presupposing and inventing a "we." Firstly, of course God is not absent from this text, and is rarely absent from constitutions or declarations that inaugurate sovereignty. Secondly, the statement from Scruton that *there is* a pre-contractual "we," a genuine membership, and the statement that what is *decided* in the Declaration is the bond of membership, collide with one another. Indeed, the very substance of the Declaration is this collision, but the admission of this fact does not resolve the difficulty.

Jacques Derrida's commentary on the same text thus serves as something of a reminder, if not as a corrective.

> There was no signer, by right, before the text of the Declaration, which itself remains the producer and guarantor of its own signature. With this fabulous event, with this fable that implies the structure of the trace and is indeed only possible by means of the inadequation of a present to itself, a signature gives itself a name. It opens *for itself* a line of credit, *its* own credit for itself *to* itself.[10]

It is correct to say that the Declaration must presuppose a "we," the "people." But presupposition is not the same thing as existence. That is why the Declaration remains a contract, opening a line of credit. It promises what it does not have. It promises that henceforth, from the present until the future, we the people shall be constituted. In this structure of the promise theology enters. For Scruton it is territory that makes this promise possible. Territory is the material fact behind the promise of the people to itself. But, in the case of the formation of the United States, this territorial "we" is constructed from a set of territories. These days the causes of the American Civil War tend to mean that those opposing the secessionists are understood as defending the just cause. Yet the uniting of the states, the decision to invent a new territorial jurisdiction, would almost certainly never have occurred if agreeing to a new Constitution meant giving up the right to secede. It is unclear that those state representatives who agreed to this unification saw it as an act of genuine membership, rather than as a worthwhile conventional arrangement.

It is just as valid to insist that "the people" are invented in the Declaration as it is to say that the Declaration assumes their pre-existence. The impossibility of deciding between these possibilities means that what is inaugurated, what is promised, is always in need of confirmation. That "a people" *are* always remains finally to be confirmed. No foundation of democratic law can ever avoid this paradox and the need it produces. Democracy remains haunted by the uncertainty of its origins. To make "territorial jurisdiction" the true bond that truly binds the people is to give this phrase the same meaning as the God that authorizes religious membership.

Those who make declarations that found democracies are *never* the people themselves. If the people are always in each case invented by the declaration that binds them together under a jurisdiction, then the people cannot be author of the declaration. And indeed they are not. It is always *someone* or *some group* who declares, on behalf of the whole group, the whole group that is *to be constituted*. That which inaugurates the people is not the people itself. The act that founds democracy is never itself an act *of* democracy, never an act *from within* a democracy, nor within a people who grant themselves a democratic jurisdiction.

This thought transforms the question of whether democracy is exportable. Never coming "from the people themselves," democracy is always and *must* always be given *from the outside*. No foundation of democracy from the inside, by a member, is possible. Democracy is *only* exportable. Does it make a difference whether the person who founds a democracy intends to be a member of the group that is being founded? Does it matter whether the founder agrees to be bound by the jurisdiction that is inaugurated? Probably. The imposition upon a population of "democratic" rule by somebody bound to *another* sovereignty does not seem the same thing as proclaiming a new law and the abolition of the rule by which *they themselves* have been bound. Yet the point remains unassailable that even in this latter case, the act of foundation is something that always emerges from the "outside." Australian democracy, for example, was the result of English donation, of a legislative decision in England to grant Australia a new, democratic sovereignty. And thus, even if the founder is outside what is founded, it is not clear that the outcome is *necessarily* less democratic.

Crime and miracle

Foundation has an aporetic relationship to time. The act of foundation conjoins past and present, in that it presupposes the past existence of what it also invents in the present. The group is invented with the fable that inaugurates it, yet the *form* of the fable is necessarily that the members *already* belonged to one another, at least sufficiently to agree to be bound in the declarative event. Foundation is presupposition. On the other hand, foundation joins the present and the future. Because the act of foundation opens a line of credit, because it promises what it does not have, it effectively claims that what it does not yet have will indeed be given. That is why the act of foundation requires constant confirmation. The "legitimacy" of the act that inaugurates the law is never certain. That a constitution is promulgated is never certain on the day that it is promulgated. There is always the chance that it will be an act without significance or force, just a person reading a piece of paper that does not in fact produce any successful fable of membership at all.

On 9 November 1918, for instance, Philipp Scheidemann proclaimed a new social democratic republic for Germany in Weimar, the Weimar republic. But what precipitated the proclamation was the *prior* proclamation on the same day in Berlin by Karl Liebknecht that henceforth Germany was a socialist republic. Two declarations intended to inaugurate a territorial jurisdiction were thus made on the very same day, and a maximum of one could turn out to be "true." Yet both depend on proclaiming that they are true from that moment forth. The problem this raises is obvious: when is a declaration *actual*? Five minutes after Scheidemann's proclamation, the Weimar republic could not have been said with any certainty whatsoever to exist, just as it was not possible to say for certain that Liebknecht's socialist republic was stillborn. But if not then, then when? When an election is held, when a parliament is convened, when police succeed in arresting and prosecuting people on the basis of the new legal regime? If the certainty is not there at the inaugurating moment, which it never can be, then it is never finally certain. Is one year of the Weimar republic – a state detested by a large portion of its members from its inception – enough to ensure that it really does exist? Perhaps fifteen years of democracy does not make it real. Perhaps the entire history of that republic was only a quasi-existence, haunted by the spectre of the government that followed it. Rather than the birth of democracy, perhaps the proclamation of the Weimar republic was only the birth of the midwife of National Socialism.

Not all democratic foundation is as shaky as the German revolution of 1918. And the history of all democracies is not as catastrophic as the fate of that republic. But what is revealed by the fact that two republics could be proclaimed for the same territory on the same day is true for all democratic proclamations, for all foundation of territorial jurisdiction. And that is the violence of all foundation, a violence that necessarily haunts what it founds. Violence here does not necessarily refer to spilt blood. It is a matter of disrupting what preceded foundation. If what is founded begins at the moment of foundation, then the Weimar proclamation was violent in relation to the Berlin proclamation it was intended to forestall. It was a proclamation, a fabulous event, that was necessarily *illegitimate* in relation to that which preceded it. That after all is the meaning of foundation, an event that begins something new, something not accounted for by what already exists. This violence, this absence of legitimacy, does not mean that all democracies are illegitimate. But their legitimacy lies not in their past but in their future. As such, this legitimacy is never finally certain, never quite enough, and always in want of further confirmation.

In other words, what is indistinguishable is whether democracy begins with the originary crime or the originary miracle. The same event is describable with both terms. Democracy never begins "democratically." Law never begins "legitimately." If they cannot begin democratically or legally, then the fact that democracy or law can begin at all, if they ever do, is miraculous. As long as the foundational and presuppositional structure is necessary for the beginning of democracy, then this beginning is strictly impossible.

And yet there are territories that call themselves democracies. In each case a miraculous fable, a myth, is involved.

Whether a constitution or an electoral system emerges from a declaration of independence and a general congress, or whether it is engineered "on behalf of" a population by an imported team of constitutional lawyers working hand in hand with an imported army, this double perspective is always equally possible. Whether it is a matter of Iraq today, or of the uniting in federation of the American states, the fact remains: whether it is crime or miracle is always undecidable, and always in the process of being decided. And that is why a religious blessing is almost always attributed to the foundational act. In that way an authorship is presumed that is not open to challenge by mortals. Of course, the *attribution* of divine sanction for an act of foundation *is* potentially open to challenge by mortals. In spite of this, however, those proclaiming political foundation usually feel compelled to add such a layer of *external* sovereign authority to their own declarative act.

Antigone

A final return to *Antigone*. What is the essence of the tragedy? Her two brothers dead, Antigone resolves to bury Polynices – the traitor to the city – in spite of Creon's prohibition against this very burial. Scruton argues that the conflict between Creon and Antigone represents that between political order and religious duty. This latter conflict is, he concludes, strictly unresolvable:

> Public interest has no bearing on Antigone's decision to bury her dead brother, while the duty laid by divine command on Antigone cannot possibly be a reason for Creon to jeopardize the state.[11]

The conflict is thus staged as that between public and private, between the universal and the specific, where the *religious* is identified with the latter terms. The divine rule is private, singular, idiomatic, whereas the sovereign law of the city is public and universal. But does not the divine duty think itself as necessary, as applying to all *its* members, just as human law applies to every citizen? Is it not just the fact that Antigone, a private citizen, is acting against Creon, against the "state," that makes her decision private?

Scruton's reading of *Antigone* thus already decides between religion and politics. It has already decided to think human, "public" law as *the* law, and religious duty merely a matter of conscience, of the private "choice" of each citizen? Such a reading refuses to grant the religious its own terms, and sees the tragedy in terms of the modern "political" separation of the theological and the secular. The tragedy is then grasped as an illustration of the consequences of a state that is religiously intolerant. But this intolerance is not understood in such a reading as failing to recognize the *fact* of (religious) law beyond the sovereignty of the state. Rather, Creon's crime is simply to make law that intrudes too far into the "private sphere," and thereby steps upon our "rights" to a "free choice" concerning our beliefs.

Scruton describes the conflict of the tragedy as that between public (secular) law, and private (religious) law. If this already "takes sides" against religious law, nevertheless he does describe the conflict as unresolvable. In this sense he does take the position of Antigone seriously, as ordained by some kind of law. He writes: "the duty laid by divine command on Antigone." But this too requires further examination. The main supporting text for describing Antigone's actions as determined by divine command is her statement beginning at line 450 of the Loeb edition of the tragedy:

> Yes, for it was not Zeus who made this proclamation, nor was it Justice who lives with the gods below that established such laws among men, nor did I think your proclamations strong enough to have power to overrule, mortal as they were, the unwritten and unfailing ordinances of the gods.[12]

Here Antigone argues that the human, mortal laws of Creon were not proclaimed by either the upper or lower gods, implying that by contrast her own actions are determined religiously. Most translations interpret the text this way. Both Martin Heidegger and Jacques Lacan, however, insist that a literal reading of Sophocles makes it clear that Antigone refers not to the basis of Creon's actions, but to her own. It is *her own* decision to bury her brother that Antigone insists *is not* based in proclamations of Zeus or the lower god Justice (Dike). Lacan explains the matter this way:

> She says clearly, "You [Creon] made the laws." But once again the sense is missed. Translated word for word, it means, "For Zeus is by no means the one who proclaimed those things to me." Naturally, she is understood to have said – and I have always told you that it is important not to understand for the sake of understanding – "It's not Zeus who gives you the right to say that." But she doesn't, in fact, say that. She denies that it is Zeus who ordered her to do it. Nor is it *Dike*, which is the companion or collaborator of the gods below. She pointedly distinguishes herself from *Dike*. "You have got that all mixed up," she, in effect, says. "It may even be that you are wrong in the way you avoid the *Dike*. But I'm not going to get mixed up in it; I'm not concerned with all these gods below who have imposed laws on men."[13]

Justice, Dike, is the god who has given man the possibility of founding human law. Thus Antigone does not refer to this god in order to justify her actions. Nor does she refer to Zeus, to the upper gods, the gods proper. All these are merely the authorities that lie behind the mortal laws of humans. They are the means for justifying the decision to institute and implement laws on earth. She herself does not rely on such grounds.

Such a translation, then, undoes the possibility of understanding the tragedy as the conflict between politics and religion. The laws of the state are *already* tied to and involved with divine sanction, whereas Antigone's actions exceed the law of both mortals and immortals. What then *is* the meaning of Antigone's decision? Perhaps it is the decision itself that must give us a hint toward its possible meaning. Antigone's decision is to bury her brother. The burial of Polynices has been prohibited on the grounds that he is the enemy of the state, and Creon's edict means that his corpse must be left as decomposing carrion for any beast to devour. The fate handed to him by Creon's decree is thus less human than that reserved for even the worst ordinary criminal. Even the criminal receives a burial. Even the criminal receives this ritual that acknowledges that one who no longer formerly existed. Polynices is denied this ritual and its conclusion, the grave that marks the absence of the one who has died.

Here is how Lacan interprets the meaning of this prohibition and Antigone's refusal to accept it:

> The fact that it is man who invented the sepulchre is evoked discreetly. One cannot finish off someone who is a man as if he were a dog. One cannot be finished with his remains simply by forgetting that the register of being of someone who was identified by a name has to be preserved by funeral rites. [. . .] Because he is abandoned to the dogs and the birds and will end his appearance on earth in impurity, with his scattered limbs an offense to heaven and earth, it can be seen that Antigone's position represents the radical limit that affirms the unique value of his being without reference to any content, to whatever good or evil Polynices may have done, or to whatever he may be subjected to.[14]

Creon's law denies Polynices his very existence. Creon has exceeded the bounds of human law, but that does not mean he has trespassed on divine jurisdiction. Rather, he has misunderstood the origin of the possibility of mortal law as such. And that origin is the very fact of mortality. Law begins from the fact of mortality. Being mortal means that man is condemned to his own, singular existence. Each one dies alone. It is this mortal solitude that necessitates that way of being with others that is called law.

Burial is the mark of this singular mortality of each individual, regardless of the form his or her life took. Burial is the means of remembering the dead, a mechanism for *marking* the absence of somebody at a particular site. But burial is also the means that permits the work of mourning to take place, that makes it possible for the living in effect to forget the dead in favor of life. Without burial the dead may be neither remembered nor forgotten. The thought of law emerges from a need of each, mortal individual, faced with mortality, to find a way of being with others, a way of avoiding mortal dangers and of finding a common way of being together. The law of burial, then, is not merely one law amongst the diversity of human laws. The burial rite, and the grave, the crypt, are the signs of the very possibility and necessity of law as such, in the singular existence of each mortal individual.

Antigone's decision to bury her brother and thereby to condemn herself to a mortal fate is the decision to take upon herself the necessity of recognizing the singular mortality of the individual. It is not that she is involved in a "genuine bond of membership" with Polynices, even though she apparently justifies her actions on the basis of blood in common. Even if this is why it is *in this case* that she makes this sacrificial decision, nevertheless the *meaning* of the decision, of the tragedy, concerns the singularity of each individual in relation to the foundation of law.

Creon forgets that law involves each individual in their being. This forgetting is proper to law itself, just as it is part of the function of burial to enable the work of mourning that allows "ordinary" life to return for the bereaved. Indeed, the "universalism" of law necessitates the "transcendence" of the "private," of the singular. Yet the law begins with this singularity each time, with the mortality of each of its "members." And thus singularity is proper to law, even the most universal law. Rather than a genuine bond, the law is founded on the very absence of a bond, on the mortal fact, the fact that each individual *is* an individual *because* they are each consigned to their own mortality. What Creon denies, what Antigone takes upon herself, is that the foundation of law is the mortal existence of all those who are thereby destined to remain strangers to each other.

In other words, the possibility of law does not arise from the "belonging together" implied in membership or territory. It is the very fact of not belonging together, of each being mortal for themselves, of necessarily being strangers to one another, that necessitates inventing a way of being together that we call law. The problem is that recognizing this fact does not overcome the problem of law. Law does not solve the problem of sovereign singularity. Antigone is not the example that dictates a proper politics. She is not the figurehead of a proper law. There is no way of politically taking Antigone "into account" in order to resolve the fact that law, founded on mortality, is dedicated to the living. Polynices is like the man chosen in the "selections" at Auschwitz: condemned to a mortal fate, utterly divorced from any acknowledgment of the fact of his existence. It is doubtful that any politics can find proper legitimacy in the fact that there have been people condemned to this fate. The foundation of law is the necessity of avoiding such a situation, yet the singular origin of law means that it can never provide any certainty or guarantee of this.

All law, whether democratic or not, is founded upon the suppression of the singularity of the mortals to whom it applies. All legal or democratic foundation, therefore, however well it is intended, carries with it the risk that *its* singular foundation may imply that another individual, or several, or many, are silently consigned to an unacknowledged oblivion. No proclamation or declaration that inaugurates a jurisdiction can occur without risking violence in relation to another singularity. Nothing can ever guarantee that a law or a democracy that is begun with a declarative act does not thereby violently assert itself in the face of an other. That there is democracy or law, if there ever is, is always a matter of an originary miracle and an originary crime.

Chapter 3

Sorry We Killed You

Of course, it is not a matter of rejecting or excluding reconciliation. [. . .] So if forgiveness has a finality, if it is given in view of reconciliation, that is, of being at peace with the other or, as they say in the Truth and Reconciliation Commission, of "healing away" the traumatic experience, if forgiveness has such a finality, then it is not pure, gracious, and unconditional forgiveness. Let us come back to the situation of the world today. Speaking of this equivocal use of the word "forgiveness," we see that all these political scenes of forgiveness, of asking for forgiveness and repentance, are often strategic calculations made in view of healing away. I have nothing against that. I have something against the use of the word "forgiveness" to describe these cases.

Jacques Derrida[1]

It is not only politicians who like to characterize Australia as the land of the "fair go." Many Australians of varying political stripes who trade in the currency of cultural capital are attracted to this self-assessment. It conveys a sense less of moral rectitude than of a kind of innate generosity of spirit, or at least willingness to withhold judging others until all the cards have been dealt. In celebrating the fair go, Australians portray themselves as fundamentally relaxed about the doings of others, as tolerant. The very need to paint such a picture, however, reflects less its veracity than a wish for projecting an image. The image is defensive. "We are patient in the judgment of others," means, really, "Do not judge us." It is in fact a threat to those who may judge. "Judge us," the ethic of the fair go implicitly says, "and you show yourself to *be* other than us, to be un-Australian." Such an ethic is self-protective and concealing, amounting to an agreement not to discuss one another's sins. Extending the right to a fair go amounts to an injunction to each to mind their own business.

This is not quite like a gangster's code, to withhold all moral judgment for the sake of our mutual family business. The ethic of the fair go also carries the sense that it reaches a limit, the limit of judgment. There is a strange duplicity in Australian attitudes to law. A culture that idolizes Ned Kelly is also frequently prepared, for instance, to shout hysterical abuse at those who ride bicycles without a helmet. What is the source of this outrage? Is it just the opportunity to judge somebody as committing a stupid and dangerous infraction of the legal code, or is it the fury that, were I to hit you with my car and render a fatal head injury, it is *I* and not you who will *unfairly* suffer most? Unethical others may always try to abuse my ethic of the fair go, to take advantage of my preparedness to grant the benefit of the doubt. Therefore, holding to the ethics of the fair go also means reserving the right *to* judge. And to judge harshly, for what remains intolerable is the abuse of my tolerance. Behind the apparently easygoing code of understanding lies a sense of pending moral outrage and vengeance. The veneer of tolerance is a means of granting to oneself the right to proclaim the limits of tolerance.

In other words, the ethic of the fair go means two things. It means, firstly, an agreement not to probe too deeply into the possible sins of others. I will not ask where you got yours, so long as you do not ask where I got mine. It means, secondly, holding on to the right to a kind of moral fury, at those who threaten what I say is mine, who threaten what I have managed to get hold of. It is perhaps still not that far from a convicts' code. It is the convict mentality in the sense of an agreement not to ask one another of what crimes we were convicted. Furthermore, this agreement is the means by which we, the convicts, can remain in solidarity against those who constantly threaten to take away our meagre possessions and privileges. Behind the ethic of the fair go in Australian society lies the feeling that there are things we would prefer you didn't bring up.

The convict rarely feels a sense of guilt about the crimes for which he is convicted, because from his perspective it is almost always a crime of necessity, or at least an accident of circumstance.

Yet there remains the feeling of being judged from above, and this is a feeling not only of resentment but of fear. To speak about our crimes is to admit that we are capable of being judged. And to admit the possibility of being judged is to admit the possibility of doing justice, to admit the horrifying possibility that justice may be done to us. Perhaps this exposes a characteristic of the Australian "psyche" that has been passed down since the days of the penal colony. But if this is the case, it is *also* the case that the ethic of the fair go conceals a hole in Australian public morality. And that hole, before it is anything else, is the history of the treatment of the indigenous population from settlement until today. In recent years, some of these unmentionable sins have emerged into visibility, and the way in which this has happened bears an uncanny resemblance to the narrative of a ghost story.

The Sixth Sense

The movie *The Sixth Sense* seems, from its lighting, its music, and its advertising, to be a horror film.[2] The audience is led to believe that when they sit down in the dark theatre to watch *The Sixth Sense* they can anticipate *horror*, because what they see bears the generic marks of a ghost story. Many early sequences evoke the fear that comes with the realization that the apparently mundane world is in fact haunted. Yet as *The Sixth Sense* unfolds, this set-up is dissipated. It gradually dawns on the audience that the film intends to lead them *out* of the world of horror, past their fears, and towards some better, more uplifting, awareness. *The Sixth Sense* is a film concerned with the moral improvement of its audience. It is an anti-horror movie in the guise of a horror movie. The message of *The Sixth Sense* is that our fears and our fascination with the ghosts of the past are overly morbid, and that the everyday world is not nearly as horrifying as we allow ourselves to imagine or desire. It is not trying to dispel the belief in spectres, but rather to educate us toward a healthier attitude toward the spectral.

What is a ghost? In *The Sixth Sense*, as elsewhere, a ghost is the ethereal remains of someone who has died. But, more specifically, a ghost is a remnant of a person whose death was unjust, and where this injustice has not come to the light of day or been avenged. Because the crime has not been remembered, or because justice has not been done, the ghost remains unsettled, in a medial world between the mortal realm and the heavenly kingdom. Ghosts remain visible, but not to everybody, requiring sensitivity to perceive their presence. Most people, most of the time, are overly concerned with the material reality that most closely surrounds them, with the everyday business of living, and with this concern comes a loss of sensitivity to other realms and other kinds of beings.

In the early part of the film, the little boy who can see ghosts experiences one terrifying scene after another of these "presences" from the past. We understand that he is more sensitive than most. At his school, for example, he sees a vision of several black men hanging by their necks. When he mentions to his teacher that he knows about people who were murdered in his school-building many decades ago, he is told that this is impossible. There is no record of any such murders. He is told, essentially, that such visions are the product of the overactive imagination of a child. But we understand that what the boy sees did actually occur, and that he alone is aware of the racial crimes of the past, even if he does not grasp their meaning. The audience is thereby given clear signs of what ghosts mean. That there are ghosts means that we live today with a *sense* of crimes past, crimes that are not only personal but social, that we may no longer know or *bother* to investigate, but which have contributed to the making of the present world, and for which we therefore continue to bear some responsibility. This sense that we are responsible for unknown past crimes is the very meaning of the sixth sense.

The turning point of *The Sixth Sense* could not be clearer. The boy is haunted and terrified by the presence of ghosts that only he seems able to perceive. But then it is suggested that perhaps, rather than a *danger* to the boy, the ghosts are in fact seeking his aid. The ghosts, which appear threatening, in fact *need us*, the living. The movie thereby announces its agenda: not a horror movie, but a piece of moral education or social therapy. The boy realizes his task is to bring to public light the unjustly forgotten and unacknowledged crimes of the past, in order that the ghosts may finally rest.

This is his task, yet we *do not* see the boy assisting the ghosts he has already seen earlier in the film. Rather, these earlier ghosts are forgotten, and a new ghost is suddenly introduced, the ghost of a little girl. This girl has only very recently died, and is about to be buried. What the girl's father does not know is that she was murdered by her own mother. But the little boy, led by the ghost of the girl to a crucial videotape, is able to reveal this truth to the father. The father has lost his daughter, but at least he understands who is responsible for this loss. An incomprehensible catastrophe is explained, opening the possibility for the proper work of justice. And hence the girl, who now knows that her loving father understands the crime that led to her death, and that a criminal prosecution can now be anticipated, is able to cease haunting the present.

The Sixth Sense intends to show us that the ghosts of the past are not to be feared, but are instead a call to us to respond. Rather than blindly and fearfully denying their existence, ghosts are asking us to come to terms with the terrible facts of the past, for their sake and ours. In the guise of a horror movie, *The Sixth Sense* offers us a narrative in which we learn that it is up to us, those living today, to look clearly at our own past in order to live more justly. The problem with *The Sixth Sense* is that this moral lesson is taught precisely by doing what it is telling us *not* to do. It calls upon us to remember, but it works by forgetting.

The movie itself forgets its own past, because it does not know *how* to deal with it. The boy does *not* try to undo the injustice of the hanged black men haunting his school. These deaths are utterly forgotten, relegated to a "horror scene" at the beginning of the movie. For how, decades upon decades later, would justice be able to be done in this case? All the perpetrators are dead, the records probably do not exist, and if they did, is there any way such information could be used to render justice? When the crime is homicide, and when it occurred so long ago that even the murderers are dead, is it ever really possible for those who remain alive to respond to these crimes in a way that achieves "justice"? What if we cannot imagine what a just response to the discovery of past murders might be? This question exposes why ghosts are frightening, because they threaten the notions of justice with which we normally operate.

The real threat of the ghost is that we might not be able to imagine an answer to such questions.

The Sixth Sense does not pursue the horrifying implications of the realization that there may not be any way of rendering justice for the violent crimes of the past. Rather, the movie forgets them at the moment it asks us to remember, by allowing the boy to "solve" a more recent crime. And when he is alerted to the murder of the girl by her ghost there is, due to incredible luck, compelling evidence right at hand: a videotape. The possibility for justice is dependent upon a miraculous mechanism for exposing the truth that will get the machinery of law going.

The movie *seems* to expose the horrifying fact that violent crimes can be utterly forgotten, the horrifying possibility that we may be murdered without any kind of retribution, the horrifying realization that *time* may intervene so that justice is impossible or comes too late to be effective. In fact, however, *The Sixth Sense* flees the horror of such possibilities by conveniently forgetting its own premises. *The Sixth Sense* shirks the irresponsible fascination with ghosts in your "average" horror movie, yet this "moral" stand depends on the very immorality it rejects. In the guise of a call to remember the violent crimes of the past, it actually finds itself needing to forget the worse crime. And, furthermore, to heal the wounds of those violent crimes it *does* "remember," it concocts mechanisms for exorcising ghosts that work to make justice miraculously attainable.

Apologies

Is this not precisely the situation in which Australia found itself in relation to the "stolen generation"? This issue in Australian public affairs – that many Aboriginal children were removed from their parents throughout much of the twentieth century in order to be "assimilated" among white families – produced a great division in Australia. These "crimes" went unrecognized by any legal authority throughout the period in which they were conducted. Those responsible for these policies, and those carrying them out, felt their actions justified. They undoubtedly believed they were acting in the best interests of the children. Child protection is a responsibility of government, and it would be criminal not to act according to what one believes this responsibility demands. If these actions were truly criminal, it was a criminality of which the perpetrators were unaware. It was a criminal misunderstanding of the responsibility with which the perpetrators were charged, a failure to keep the promise implied in accepting the responsibility of governing and protecting.

Only a change in society meant that such policies could, *now*, be understood widely to be crimes. A redefinition of the acts had to occur, and thus it was not exactly the case that these crimes were unknown. The exposure of these "crimes" was then *something like* the revealing of a secret, but a secret that at the same time was widely known. Or, even, what was at stake was a series of actions and policies that were not even kept secret, because they were simply past actions of government agencies concerned with child welfare. They simply fell into a state of being forgotten.

The division produced by the report on the stolen generation was thus not really about the nature of the acts at all. A new consensus, today's consensus, agreed that these were scandalous crimes. Rather, the division was provoked by the question of how to *respond* to the exposure of the injustice and violence of these acts. More specifically, the matter in question was whether a governmental apology was necessary or wise. Both sides of this division were in agreement that crimes had been committed and forgotten by Australian society, even at the moment of being perpetrated. There was consensus too that it is a good thing that such matters are investigated and exposed to the public. Yet the focus on this issue, and the protracted public debate about the necessity for a government apology, revealed more about the nature of Australian society than simply the gravity of the issue.

The "stolen generation," despite its violence and its importance, is flanked on either side by crimes the violence of which will not be ameliorated by any apology. On the one hand, there is the original crime, the invasion of the land, and the many murders and severe oppression that accompanied colonization and made Australian democracy possible. All of the debate by historians about the specifics of the European invasion of Australia and its consequences are overshadowed by the knowledge that murder was common, and that the opponent was in an essentially helpless position. The presupposition of *Terra Nullius* is a legal fiction that serves to mask a dark reality.

On the other hand, there is the *present* crime, the fact that this history of oppression is still today reflected in the dire circumstances of the vast majority of the remaining Aboriginal population. Extraordinary mortality rates, unemployment rates, alcohol and drug addiction rates, and incarceration rates are only those facts most available for statistical analysis, amongst all the problems faced by the descendants of the original inhabitants. Any honest moral conscience has trouble coping with this present situation, first of all because it remains far from certain how to undo the injustice of these circumstances. Despite large sums being spent on indigenous health, despite efforts at fostering indigenous self-government, little has improved. Either even larger sums must be spent, or new strategies must be devised.

And throughout any reflection upon this history of failure there is the hard realization that no federal election has ever been influenced to any significant degree by such questions. If white Australia has shown little interest in exploring the unsavory details of the invasion that is called "settlement," it has even less concern for the crimes of the present. There is virtually no group anywhere in the developed world in a comparable situation to the Australian Aborigines, but for the most part the nation is only slightly troubled. Most Australian citizens are at best *hopeful* that welfare arrangements at least prevent the most horrific outcomes, and comfort themselves that surely things must at least be heading in a more positive direction.

The call for a governmental apology for the stolen generation, however well-meaning, is, among other things, an attempt to flee *those* crimes that offer little prospect of any just response. The crimes involved in settlement and the crime that is the contemporary situation of the indigenous population are in some way avoided by directing one's political attention and outrage at the "stolen generation." This is the case even if it is one of the issues that contribute to that current condition. The very notion of the "stolen generation" treats a largely still living group as though they were ghosts, the remnants of crimes from long ago, the forgotten. Yet they are also crimes that are recent enough, well-documented enough, that they can now be brought to the light of day, remembered, and some kind of justice rendered. As an "indigenous issue," the stolen generation succeeds in bridging the divide between the forgotten crimes of the past, and the continuing suffering of the living. This breeds the notion that, if not for the intractability of a heartless Prime Minister, reconciliation with these living ghosts might still today be possible. The apology, therefore, is treated by many of its proponents as the miraculous mechanism for a proper, just, exorcism.

The idea of an apology, furthermore, like *The Sixth Sense*, contains the thought that these ghosts are calling us to respond, that it is up to us to give a sign, and that with such a sign the possibility of justice arises. But whether "we" give or do not give signs, such a gesture cannot "achieve" reconciliation, nor overcome the tragedy of past crimes. Whether a crime is or is not forgiven is not a matter for the perpetrator but for the victim. The criminal may offer remorse, but it is up to the victim to decide whether this remorse is sincere. Furthermore, *even if remorse is sincerely expressed*, it is still up to the victim to either accept or reject any apology offered.

In *this* case, an "apology" would be delivered not by the individual "criminals" themselves, but by the government, on the understanding that it bears responsibility for past crimes. The notion is that a government is one subject across time, in effect a sovereign and continuing subjectivity. Despite being comprised of different people, then, the government continues, as *one being* in itself, to bear responsibility for its prior activities. The problem is this: even if one accepts the notion that government continues to be *responsible* for its actions from decades past, how is it possible for a government composed of entirely different people to be *sincere* in its apology?

There is a predictable retort to the implication of such a question. If the feelings of those who make an apology *on behalf of* the government are *sincere*, then the apology itself is sincere. This is too simple. At stake is a difference between the feeling of shame and the capacity to apologize. That one is a member of a government or a society that committed acts one considers shameful, and that one sees the connection between those acts and one's own position in the present, may induce shame. Where one sees the connections from past to present, responsibility too is borne. Against those who maintain simply that no apology can be given because "we" did not do it, it must be confessed that responsibility is a more complex phenomenon than that. Children who become wealthy because of thefts committed by their parents or grandparents carry responsibility for these thefts because of the benefits the children receive from the sins of their forebears, benefits that could have been another's. In the same way, if during the period of National Socialism Volkswagen relied upon Jewish slave labor, then the subsequent executives of that corporation continue to bear responsibility for those crimes, because their present fortune is in some way the outcome of that past.

But being responsible is not the same thing as having the capacity to apologize. This point is subtle but not pedantic. If responsibility *can* be inherited, this is because each person is responsible for *who they are*, and for the situation that allows them to be who they are. That is why it is possible to say that all those who live prosperously in the developed world carry responsibility for the poverty of the third world. The responsibility comes from the fact of the situation itself, even if most people can in no way consider themselves the author of that situation.

Responsibility may provoke shame, but it is not the same thing as the ability to apologize. It is not possible to apologize for acts one has not oneself committed. It is not possible to apologize *on behalf of* somebody else. An apology cannot be offered for one's responsibility for a situation, but only for the acts one has oneself committed. It is not possible to apologize for what one's father has done, or for the fortune of one's birth. It is possible to admit responsibility and shame, but to apologize *for* one's parents is to twist the meaning of apology. With this twist the apology becomes disingenuous. The claim that to refuse an apology is cold or heartless does not undo the falseness of the logic behind the call.

Reconciliation

It is therefore utterly questionable whether it is possible for a government – subject to a political campaign, to a *demand* – to *genuinely* offer its remorse for crimes of decades past. Even more questionable is the idea that an apology will achieve reconciliation. To demand an apology is of course not the same thing as the claim that with an apology reconciliation will be achieved. But in the *campaign* for an apology this is the claim that was *in effect* being made. The campaign functioned in a way that constantly *implied* that the *refusal* to apologize was what prevented forgiveness and hence reconciliation. It is not that an apology necessarily demands or produces forgiveness. Yet the political meaning of the *call* for an apology was the assertion that holding back an apology is what prevents the *achievement* of reconciliation.

As this campaign dragged on, and as it became clearer that no apology would be forthcoming, the reasoning of those conducting the campaign adjusted itself. The campaign was, not entirely but largely, a matter of the non-indigenous population speaking among themselves. The greater the shame heaped upon the government for its stubborn refusal to apologize, the more it became clear that the call for an apology was, whatever else it was, a move within a party political game. And hence the clearer it became that the incessant call to apologize was not being made because of what it might *achieve* for the indigenous population, but as a means of attacking the government. The "issue" of the apology seemed increasingly to be a distraction from the contemporary difficulties faced by the Aboriginal community.

As the possibility dawned that to continue demanding an apology might come at a political cost for the federal opposition, the claim became a little more desperate. Those calling for the apology began deploying a different logic, arguing that an apology was necessary in order to allow a "line to be drawn" under the "issue." An apology became necessary in order to "move on" to other issues, to "bring closure" to the debate, and hence the function of an apology as a mechanism for *forgetting* became apparent. To apologize, to ask for forgiveness, in order to overcome a difficult issue, in order therefore to forget it, is, in truth, not a matter of apologizing at all, but of wishing for a world where certain matters did not arise.

The truth of this relation between an apology and the *forgetting* of the crime for which an apology is being demanded, is the concept of "reconciliation" itself. It is true to argue that reconciliation is a "symbolic" concept, that it is really a matter of marks and signs, of treaties and agreements, of reciprocal symbolic gestures by governments, by "publics," by community "representatives" and community "leaders," indigenous and non-indigenous. Reconciliation means putting into motion a technics of agreement. What is remarkable is the frequency with which non-indigenous people will admit that reconciliation is symbolic, and then defend the concept on the grounds of the efficacy of symbols. Such arguments are fantastic. They are the consequence of the difficulty of finding solutions for any of the problems currently facing the population they hope to reconcile with. The work of reconciliation is the work of forgetting itself.

Perhaps forgetting is necessary, but *if so* it is necessary for the indigenous population. And the *question* of its necessity is a question for the indigenous population. The criminal cannot demand reconciliation from the victims. It is a matter for the latter to decide upon, in their own terms, in their own time, with their own debate, and in their own way. The criminal is in an *essentially* passive position in relation to this question. He can perform public rituals and gestures of repentance if he chooses, and perhaps is wise to do so, but if there is forgiveness, and if it is genuine, it is for the crime itself, not for the symbols that follow it. Reconciliation, if there is such a thing, cannot be a matter of forgiving those later generations *because* they have given sufficient tokens of regret. Such gestures of repentance, if they are not mechanical, may constitute a promise – to undo the damage, to behave otherwise in the future – but if they are the reason for forgiveness, then it is not a crime that is forgiven, but an agreement to settle for the sake of the future.

True reconciliation, if there is any, is an act of forgiveness toward those original perpetrators, and acceptance of the reality of what was done, and of the reality of the situation that the indigenous population occupies *as a consequence* of what was done. And it is not a matter of the gestures and symbols of the leadership of those who would accept an apology. It is a matter for the people themselves, each individually, and whether it takes years or centuries, if it ever occurs, cannot be seriously affected by a series of signs offered as part of an ongoing political and electoral strategic game. If forgiveness is genuine, it is without condition. This is proper to the structure of the concept itself. To insist upon this structure is not a harsh or cynical way to avoid offering gestures of regret. Rather, it is recognition that the question of forgiveness and reconciliation is a question for those who would, perhaps, one day, *offer* this gift, not for those who might desire it *from them.*

An apologetic planet

It is not only in Australia that the demand for an apology has been heard. In the United States the same phenomenon has transpired in relation to the Native Americans. The South Korean government has called for an apology from the Japanese government for the female slaves it kept during World War II. President Clinton offered a quasi-apology for slavery when in South Africa. The call for an apology seems to be a political or legal *development,* as though an advance had been made, or progress had been achieved, recognized in many nations and hence making its way around the globe. Apologies have become something like a policy of harm minimization in relation to drug abuse or prostitution. Instead of adopting a defensive pose in relation to those victimized by law and society, empathy and social health demand the recognition of their victimhood. Where states have acted improperly what argument can there be against an apology, where it can bring only the benefits of social healing and reconciliation?

This phenomenon needs to be accounted for with an explanation beyond legal or political progress, beyond legal or political *fashion.* Rather it is part of a more general adjustment of the understanding and practice of democracy and law. The understanding of law has changed, such that it is seen less as a matter of drawing a line between what society or God considers to be permissible and impermissible. Rather, law is a key management tool for the social health of the population of a state. And the function of government is this work of management. The understanding of democracy is thereby transformed from being the process through which a group determines its collective existence. Rather, democracy is the imperfect means for ensuring that each individual and each collectivity has its welfare and its sufferings sufficiently recognized and addressed. Democracy becomes the spectacle whereby each group clamoring for recognition is able to impose its will and its "rights" upon the management system that is the state.

No doubt good outcomes are achieved through these changes. That the health and welfare of a nation is managed better can only be a good thing. That social problems that previously were treated punitively are increasingly addressed with compassionate concern surely reduces the harm involved. Furthermore, those who argue against such changes in law, and in the relation of government to society, mostly do so out of misplaced nostalgia for an era of certain values. That is why, for the proponents of such changes, the struggle to achieve them is grasped as a battle between progressives and conservatives, where it is the latter who wish to retard social improvement.

And yet there is a problem with such transformations in the concepts of law and democracy. The problem is that what tends to be lost is the sense of democracy itself. Modern democracy has understood itself as a method, a process, through which those within a border grant themselves the maximum amount of autonomy in relation to their collective existence. Democracy may have flaws, perhaps fatal flaws in the form it currently takes, but the *idea* of democracy is difficult to surpass. But in the movement toward government as social management, the concept of democracy is increasingly sacrificed. It is sacrificed first of all on the altar of expertise. Where the problem of government becomes a matter of the optimization of management, the optimization of social health, those in possession of "scientific knowledge" and know-how are increasingly valorized. And this can be at the cost of condescension toward democratic process, which hence leads increasingly toward finding ways of bypassing this process.

Along with the trend toward conceiving government technocratically as an institution for social management comes the growth of what is called "identity politics." For technocratic reasons it is preferable to recognize *groups* of identities, in order better to manage and treat them, to alleviate their sufferings, to undo past wrongs. Departments and bodies proliferate to deal with these identities. "Peak bodies" are formed in order to identify the leadership of the various identities, the better to render aid and justice, the better to manage them. Such changes are a return to a "Platonic" conception of the state, which is not the same thing as returning to Plato. It is a return to an organic understanding of society, as divided into its various parts, each with its proper place, each receiving its due and contributing its share.

Such a thought threatens democracy, because it ends in a government that has "taken account" of everybody, that has calculated and accounted for each individual. And it has done so because each individual exists through their identity, defined according to those *recognized* groups of which they claim membership. Democracy is undermined if it becomes the process of discovering new identities in order to absorb and assimilate them to the system. Such absorption and assimilation is in fact the antithesis of democracy, whatever benefits it may indeed bring. It is the antithesis of the notion that true democracy means the possibility for unpredictable new voices to be raised. Democracy does not mean assigning a part to each group, but rather is the eternal possibility of voices raised in struggle against the division of society *into* a system of parts. It is the perpetual possibility that new wrongs will be discovered, but not the perpetual possibility that these wrongs can be undone.[3]

The worldwide trend toward apologizing and reconciling fits within this broader transformation of democracy and law. It is part of a general struggle to overcome past injustices perpetrated against identifiable groups. This struggle is sometimes conducted in the name of "healing away," sometimes with a view to economic compensation. But in any case it is usually a matter of inventing a process for forgetting the crime that one is being called to acknowledge and remember. And, grandiose as it perhaps sounds, there is a threat to democracy involved. Insofar as justice is adjusted and redefined through such apologies and reconciliations, it is increasingly conceived as a matter of what is best for the management of the groups involved, as the right to "official" recognition of each identity, even if this means the erasure and forgetting of past wrongs for the sake of a "just" future.

South Africa's Truth and Reconciliation Commission offered amnesty to those police officers, members of security forces, or government ministers, responsible for crimes conducted during apartheid. The price paid for truth, and for the offering of remorse and apologies, was the guarantee that there will be no punishment. However valuable this truth, both socially and individually for the relatives of victims of the regime, there was also real cost. The price paid was that many people were allowed to get away with murder, literally. Whether this translates into reconciliation or justice is questionable. Few concentration camp survivors under the Nazis would put much stock in an apology by the perpetrators, let alone by the German government (yet the campaign to demand compensation for Nazi crimes from governments and corporations *is* a species of the same phenomenon). There can be no expectation that such gestures produce forgiveness. Forgiveness, if there is any (and who is to say there should be?), is a matter for the victim.

Apologies may not hurt (yet is this so obvious?), but the real function of the call for governmental apologies lies elsewhere. One such function is the ability to draw a line under impropriety, to be able to state that, whatever crimes were committed in the name of the law, the future of the law remains legitimate. Mass murder threatens the legitimacy of a law that *follows* the period of extermination, if this "new law" cannot effectively prosecute the murderers of the past. In South Africa, in Nuremburg, in Rwanda, the meaning of truth and reconciliation is not the achievement of justice, but the necessity of imprinting the stamp of legitimacy upon the *new* law. The foundation of a new system of justice may require an implicit statement that, although hundreds or thousands may have got away with murder, *from now on* it will nevertheless be just to prosecute somebody for theft.

The ab-origin of Australian law

Things are a little different in Australia, where most of the mass murder took place many decades ago. Reconciliation does not mean here the stamp of legitimacy for a new law. But perhaps the difference is simply the length of time between the committing of massacres and their becoming visible. The beginning of Australian law coincides, not accidentally, with the beginning of the criminal mistreatment of the indigenous population. In Australia's case, few of the perpetrators were ever brought to justice, and they almost certainly did not even imagine themselves to be criminals. Yet the sense that current Australian law could not have begun without the subjugation of the prior inhabitants continues to haunt its legitimacy. Among other things, the call for reconciliation comes out of the sense many Australians have that the security granted through the existence of the law was paid for with the blood of thousands of those who were already here.

What was at stake in the call for an apology in relation to the stolen generation was more than simply party political fortunes. What was at stake was also the continuing sense that Australian law is founded on a crime. The stolen generation may be far removed from the crimes at the time of settlement, yet what the victims of the stolen generation represent to the campaigners for an apology is another symptom of the original crime. Those calling for an apology were really saying that, in refusing to grant an apology, Prime Minister Howard was refusing to enact the miraculous mechanism that would heal the wound at the beginning of Australian law. Refusing to unleash the miraculous apology, they were saying, Howard is consigning "*us*," those who benefit from current law, to the continuation of our inherited guilt.

The intensity of the debate about an apology for the stolen generation reflects the intensity of the need *not* to face other crimes, crimes for which the possibility of a just outcome seems impossible. Of course this debate also reflected the political motivations of those who wished for party political reasons to attack the government of the day, but the potency of this attack is itself significant. And this potency comes from the fact that with the question of an apology for the stolen generation there emerged a way of *apparently* discussing the continuing injustice experienced by the indigenous population, while in fact not treating the reality of this injustice at all. The stolen generation issue was conflated with the entire history of unjust treatment of Aborigines. The insufficiency of any apology is first of all the fact that to call for an apology is already to have failed to take the measure of the greatest crimes. Contrary to appearances, the call to apologize moves in the direction of banishing rather than exorcizing ghosts. It is a ritual that seems to prevent the return of the spectre, but in fact may itself be the means of perpetuating the state of haunting.

It may be argued, counter to such a proposition, that the "activism" of the High Court in relation to Mabo and Wik was evidence of a nation attempting to deal with the reality of its original crimes. In recognizing that Australia was not *Terra Nullius* at the time of European settlement, in recognizing "prior occupation," and in recognizing that this occupation ought to be expressed legally in certain Aboriginal entitlements in relation to land ownership, is the Court not attempting, however imperfectly, to render justice for the crimes of the past? What else – other than recognizing that rights that properly belong to the Aborigines have been denied and must be restored – could a court do, in order to *undo* such past failures?

The problem with this is the sense that, even with Mabo and Wik, ghosts are not being laid to rest, but rather reburied, because they *must* remain buried, because to take these crimes seriously, which can barely be imagined, would threaten the very court and the very government that could decide or legislate in relation to such questions. Between the High Court and the governments of Keating and then Howard there were various differences about the restoration or extinguishing of Aboriginal rights in relation to the land, but these differences were, if important, nevertheless still only relative. That there were people here before European settlement, that these people suffered, bled and died at the hands of the settlers, that this bloodshed and this suffering continue until today, and that all these facts in some sense dilute the sovereignty of Australia – all this can more or less be admitted and coped with in law. What could never be admitted, however, is the thought that, in the words of Roger Scruton, there was a "territorial jurisdiction" anywhere in Australia prior to settlement.

The proposition that there could have been Aboriginal territorial jurisdiction ought not depend on evidence that there were laws and police and judges and prisons. Surely these are not the proofs of territorial jurisdiction. Surely the various tribes and groups of Aborigines in Australia had their laws and their justice, and surely they were *here*, in this territory. Surely the laws and the justice of these tribes were wantonly violated by the settlers, without regard, without process, without consultation. Admitting such propositions does not mean that Aborigines who have retained a connection with certain parts of land retain certain rights in respect of that land, etcetera etcetera. Far beyond such compromises, it means admitting that the very institution of Australian law depends for its foundation upon ignoring and burying the existence of any *other law* that may already have been in effect here.

There was never proper transfer from the law of the Aborigines to the law of the European settlers. Beyond the ghosts of the thousands of Aborigines killed in the name of Australian colonization, the ghost that must continually be reburied is the ghost of Aboriginal law. Whether the original occupiers are granted the grace of admitting their existence, they must nevertheless remain without origin, as far as being, *on their own terms*, legal persons. However absurd the fear that the ownership of suburban blocks is threatened by such High Court decisions, this fear is symptomatic of the suspicion that, indeed, the morality and legality of invasion continues to haunt Australian law at its core.

Australian law has with Mabo and Wik been prepared to trace the genealogy of certain citizens to the Australian territory prior to the institution of the current legal system. In doing so, the law can admit that the rights of these citizens were trampled, and that legal remedy is suitable. But it has not and indeed must not extend this line of thought to the foundation of current Australian law itself. This law has its foundation and its propriety in English law, and this foundation is not susceptible to legal challenge. Aboriginal law – even if there are moments of concession, even if "we" *permit* portions of it to be *included* within "our" code of laws – will never reign again.

To admit that there was another law here before "our" law threatens to undermine the legitimacy of any present court or government. Even the most radical supporters of reconciliation and Aboriginal rights do not argue for the reinstatement of an Aboriginal regime that has been illegally usurped by an invader. This, however, is due to the practical impossibility of such a thought, rather than any compelling legal argument. In the end, the law will always resort to a circumspect appraisal of what is true in fact, even where it may seem questionable in law. The thought of Aboriginal law is inadmissible, yet the very foundations of Australian law and politics are haunted by its ghost.

The point is not that the issue of the stolen generation should not be investigated, nor that culpability for it should not be acknowledged. It is not that the High Court was wrong to decide that

Aborigines retained rights in respect to their prior occupation of the land of Australia. Rather, the point is that these *decisions*, the decisions of the High Court and the decision to campaign for an apology, reflect a certain kind of need: the sixth sense that something is amiss, that something has gone awry, from the beginning and until today. But this sense is not the same as a sense of justice. Nor is it the same as a need to remember past crimes. Rather, both the call for an apology and the decision to recognize "certain" rights in relation to land ownership are half-way measures, that remember *up to a certain point*, in order not to remember something else. They are attempts at renewing the sense of the propriety of the existence of law and the society it makes possible. But the mechanism of this renewal is the miraculous "solving" and resolving of the crimes of the past, that works by choosing only those crimes that seem available for being solved. To that extent they are about forgetting as much as they are about memory.

There may be no alternative but to mix a certain amount of forgetting and a certain amount of memory. Law *can* only begin by forgetting the impropriety, the non-legality, of its own origin. The point is that the particular form of this impropriety and this non-legality continue to affect the way in which the future of this law plays itself out. And these consequences come because what can be neither remembered nor forgotten, the ghosts in the machine of law, are truly threatening. Law needs to imagine itself as a rational whole, without missing elements, but it is haunted by what it must not perceive too well, the missing pieces of the edifice. The hole in the heart of law, the original crime that coincides with the foundation of law, without which law could not have begun, is also *positive*. It is this hole that pushes law into new forms and new possibilities, new ways of coping with its lack of totality, such as Mabo and Wik.

The violence at law's beginning, the sense that this beginning can never quite be properly *done*, keeps law in need of transformation, in need of a completion that never arrives. But the fact that this never arrives, that this original violence can never be undone or even really compensated, is also the continuation of violence. The injustice, the crime at the beginning of law, carries on, irremediably, threateningly, because it means that, from inception and endlessly into the future, the law is characterized by risk. And this risk includes the possibility that the apparent stability and steadfastness of the law will be exposed to horrific ghosts with which it cannot cope. Until that moment, the law works to manage the risk, to reduce the threat by treating the ghosts as non-existent or as everyday, by admitting a certain amount of haunting in order to dispel the sense of horror, or by inventing new ways of perpetuating itself. But the revenant always threatens to return.

Chapter 4

The Great Debate

Can one tell – that is to say, narrate – time, time itself, as such, for its own sake? That would surely be an absurd undertaking. A story which read: "Time passed, it ran on, the time flowed onward" and so forth – no one in his senses could consider that a narrative. It would be as though one held a single note or chord for a whole hour, and called it music. For narration resembles music in this, that it *fills up* the time. It "fills it in" and "breaks it up," so that "there's something to it," "something going on." [...] For time is the medium of narration, as it is the medium of life. *Thomas Mann*[1]

There is a common experience that as one ages the passage of time ineluctably accelerates. The period from one birthday to the next is for a small child akin to the passing of an aeon. For an adult, however, a birthday is frequently accompanied by a disturbing sense that yet another entire year has passed in almost no time at all. The perception of temporal passage seems determined by the frequency of significant events that interrupt the ordinary flow from one moment to the next to the next. The perception of time's rate of flow is determined by the *density* of the medium. This density is a function of the number of changes, actions, and discoveries. For a child, the story of a year may be filled with hundreds of important chapters, through which the world enters into life, and through which the child grows into the world in which it lives.

For an adult, perhaps, accommodated to the world, and even to the everyday dramas of love and career, entire decades may pass by in a moment, with few meaningful moments to fill out the vast expanses of days gone by. Even *apparently* significant events – marriage, divorce, the death of those around one – may lose their capacity for breaking up the endless flow. They become merely faint markers by which it is possible to establish a ghostly geography of one's life. The pathos and irony of this mature condition is that with the diminishing of assigned time comes a corresponding lessening of the ability to slow or even take notice of time's passage. Even if time is defined, as William Burroughs put it, as "that which runs out," the fact of mortality may not be sufficient to slow the acceleration of time's passage.[2] The scarcity of real change, of anything worthy of a new chapter, forces the narrative of life headlong into that most significant event, which the individual will not even be present to experience.

Perhaps it is the same with history, even though no one directly perceives the passing of historical time. Australia is among the youngest of nations. Even those recent creations such as FRYOM or the states left after the collapse of the USSR are in actuality much older, since history begins for the inhabitants not with such acts of state formation, but centuries ago. The formation of Bosnia-Herzegovina or Tajikistan at the end of the twentieth century is only one more moment added to a long sequence of historical events. The two hundred or so years of "Australian history," then, ought, according to such logic, have seemed like an eternity to its inhabitants. For *indigenous* Australians, perhaps, the last 200 years may have been perceived as a bad nightmare but a relatively brief one compared to the millennia of history. And those who have recently arrived, or who retain strong ties to other lands and other cultures, may refer Australian history to a different context, in which 200 years ago was only yesterday. But for the rest, for those who project themselves into an Australian identity, the period from European discovery until today may appear as dense as a child's first year.

This may be so, yet it is equally mixed with an opposite sensation, the feeling that two centuries of Australian history has been only lightly filled. Perhaps there is a geographical aspect to this experience. In a land so vast and empty, it takes time for anything important to happen. Perhaps great space diminishes the significance of temporal passage. Whether this is a meaningful suggestion or not, the feeling remains that Australian history has passed quickly from Cook to federation, through the wars of the twentieth century, until today.

Perhaps this brevity of history is due to the relative paucity of dramatic and significant events, in comparison to the wars, foreign, independent, and civil, or the periods of darkness and renaissance, suffering and prosperity, that punctuate the history of other lands. Perhaps, that is, there is an absence of mortal suffering to lend gravity to Australian history, a fortunate scarcity of massacres, epidemics, and famines. A schoolteacher of Australian history is, like the lost explorer Ludwig Leichhardt, faced with a great uncrossable desert, an uninviting terrain of low dunes and few landmarks, and certainly with little hope of finding a Lassiter's reef of historical gold. Other than the great narrative of the destruction of the original inhabitants, there are only the tales of exploration, of settlement, of Macarthur's sheep, the rum rebellion, the goldfields, the bushrangers, the depression, and the world wars, from which to draw anything with which to quench one's thirst for national drama.

Perhaps this is why what seems one of the lowest of the dunes in the desert of Australian history was able for a moment to loom like Everest waiting to be scaled. For a moment a movement arose to transform Australia, cosmetically speaking, from a constitutional monarchy to a republic, for no other reason, so it seemed, than because it was there. And at the time it seemed equally important to achieve this task by the centenary of federation, the nation's, or at least the state's, birthday.

But, as at Mann's Berghof on Davos, the isolation and insularity of the location contribute perhaps to a sense of great significance for events that only a short time later seem to have occurred in a fog that makes them difficult to recall. Having proved to be a mountain too high, the entire event and debate has, through a trick of time, faded into the oblivion of memory, almost as though it never happened. And, perhaps, it never did. Yet, when the event has lost its urgency, and its currency, it becomes possible to return to it at will and at leisure, like slides of a holiday of decades before. When removed from the dusty box in which they have been stored, such relics may just reveal subtleties of narrative that remained unnoticed at the time they were snapped.

Two sides

Were one to grant the notion of an *Aboriginal* territorial jurisdiction, a 40 000-year heritage could be claimed for its sovereignty and legitimacy. A very different historical scale would then be operating. No such claim could be made for the law that comes to Australia from England. This might be thought to form the basis for an argument against maintaining the link to England embodied in the figure of the Governor-General. A law with a heritage of tens of thousands of years is displaced by the much younger rule of a foreign invader. Does not, then, the perpetuation of this tie with England constitute a prolongation of the original crime of colonization? Would not the passing of a referendum that reconfigures the political system from a monarchical to a republican form help to undo these original crimes? Is it not necessary, in order to move forward, to sever these ties with the past? And does not the continuing existence of these legal ties demonstrate that Australian law, rather than founding itself on a properly legitimate basis, stems from the *contingency* of the fact that England, rather than Spain or some other country, decided to take possession of this land, in order to build a prison colony? Is it not as though our entire politico-legal system is thereby founded on a kind of historical joke?

Arguments for and against Australia becoming a republic are conducted essentially at cross-purposes. Those arguing for a republic rely for the most part on an intuitive sense that it is absurd for a head of state to be the monarch of another nation. The argument is therefore more or less nationalistic, but this nationalism is given a democratic veneer, by claiming that a President, as opposed to a Governor-General, will represent not a foreign monarch but the people of Australia. This is the basis for further arguments about the method of selecting a President, and in particular for the currently popular suggestion that the President ought to be elected. The degree of public participation in the appointment, it is argued, will determine the degree to which the President truly can be regarded as the Australian head of state, as the "reflection" of the Australian people, as Sir Zelman Cowen described the office.

Those arguing for a republic tend to belittle their opponents by portraying them constantly as anglophiles, motivated by an attachment to English royalty. Monarchists are portrayed by republicans as absurdly outmoded, children of the 1950s if not the nineteenth century, and as turning their backs on a necessary and inevitable future. They are thus attacked as the enemies of progress. Yet virtually no opponent of the republican cause argues publicly along such lines. One theme resonates continuously throughout anti-republican reasoning: that such changes represent a threat to the constitutional stability of the present arrangement. This is both the weakness and the strength of the monarchist position. It is the strength due to the reluctance of the Australian public to embrace constitutional change. By exploiting the Australian distrust of the motives of politicians, it is not difficult to persuade many that the essentially nationalistic arguments of republicans are not sub-stantial enough to justify the risk. If the change is merely cosmetic, then why bother? If it is a genuine transformation of the political system, then why are so few arguments presented about the benefits that change will bring? The republican response to such reasoning is, universally, to change the topic back to the absurdity of living under "foreign rule."

But the basic monarchist position – that constitutional change is inherently risky; don't fix what ain't broke – is also their weakness. It is weak because it is fundamentally a legal argument about the nuances of the balance of power under various arrangements. It is weak because for the bulk of the population the forum in which political positions are argued is television, a medium peculiarly unsuited to and uninterested in the intricacies of constitutional arrangement. Furthermore, legal argumentation is an especially alienating mode of discourse for those not inducted into the rituals of its presentation. Whatever precision is gained through years of perfecting its jargon, legal discourse pays for this precision the price of general inaccessibility. And if this inaccessibility is in general of benefit to lawyers, ensuring the necessity of their existence, it is decidedly a burden when employed as a means of persuasion for a general referendum in the televisually mediated world of modern Australian politics.

It is for this reason that monarchists during the referendum cam-paign were forced to take a gamble. On the one hand, they argued the pointlessness of "merely" changing the Governor-General into a

President, to be appointed in identical manner. Why bother? On the other hand, this tended to push the debate toward other methods of presidential appointment, including direct election, which for the monarchists could only increase the risk of political instability. In arguing for the status quo, they risked forcing the republicans into the worst of all positions. And, it might well be thought, it was only this division amongst the republicans that ensured that the Australian suspicion of political change was enough to defeat the referendum.

In short, the debate about the referendum was between the inane derision and nationalism of the republicans, and the constitutional technicalities of the monarchists. Of the two, undoubtedly the fears of the latter were the preferable, being at least based upon some kind of argument. Advocates of the republican cause, on the other hand, seem almost universally to be opportunists prepared to clutch at vulgar forms of persuasion such as nationalist scorn. This vulgarity is tantamount to self-indictment. Nevertheless, between both sides there was a failure at a public level to communicate what was at stake with the referendum question. And this failure is first of all the consequence of failing to communicate the meaning of the office of head of state.

Pictures of democracy

What is a head of state, really? Ever since the invention of liberalism, there has been a tendency to view the relation of people and government in binary terms, as an opposition. The government rules and protects the people, but the government is also what the people must be protected *from*. Even though the advent of liberalism coincides with the advent of modern parliamentary democracy, government tends always to be viewed as the actual or potential enemy of the freedoms of the individual. On the left, this takes the form of fear of authoritarian government and, on the right, fear of "big" government. The justification of this fear of government seems to be ever more confirmed as democratic governance comes more and more to seem like a nostalgic veneer, covering the brutal reality that what governs us all is an economic system-machine impervious to "the people's will." Yet this tendency to see government as opposed to the people or the individual is also what makes it difficult to grasp the meaning of the head of state.

The head of state, or the non-political monarch, viewed from the perspective of the opposition of government and people, is then understood more or less as the "people's politician," a figure who reflects the people, in whom the people can see themselves, and against whom the politicians ought to measure their actions. Rather than an anti-political conception, this view of the head of state as the non-political figurehead is actually the first step *toward* the politicization of the office. It is the first step toward the notion that the head of state has a mandate to speak on behalf of the people, as the people's conscience. But within the binary conception of the relation of people and state, there is no way to grasp what is dangerous about such a notion.

It is not a matter of questioning the possibility for a state to threaten its people. To ignore the threat that government poses to its citizens is to have taken the first big step toward totalitarianism. But where politics is *based* around this possibility, as liberalism always is, the concept of democracy becomes skewed. In fact, the kind of democracy found in representative parliamentarism is based on a *threefold* structure that reflects a delicate balance in the thought of democracy itself. Democracy, of course, means "the rule of the people." Does the word itself not suggest the kind of binarism just mentioned, between the people on the one hand, and the law or the state on the other hand? Does not modern democracy arise as the counter to the theological tyrannies of the middle ages, replacing the divine right of kingship with the idea that there is nothing above the people? That there is nothing above the people implies, logically, that the people should rule. Is this not simple and true?

The thought of democracy, however, *cannot* so quickly be identified with the notion that nothing is higher than the people. Understanding this means yet again reflecting on how any democracy is founded. Democracy begins with an event, a decision, an act, even a miracle. The act does not inaugurate the rule of a people, because the act decides that there is a people, a "we, the people," who could *become* democratic citizens. It decides that the people means *this* people *here*, not those people there. In short, it depends upon a decision about borders, which are never natural, nor neutral.

Furthermore, the foundation is never *itself* a democratic act, and it can never follow a democratic method. This is not the same thing as saying that instituting democracy may not be popular. But unless there is a *way* of measuring that popularity and then translating that measurement into an official declarative act, how can the decision to inaugurate a democracy itself be democratic? And the means of measurement, and the threshold to be reached, would themselves be matters that must already have been agreed upon in order to call such a decision democratic. And, before a democracy has begun, such agreement is obviously impossible in principle.

Another way to put it is to say that democracy begins with a "here," a "now," a "we," and a "way." In fact, the first three are part of the fourth. Democracy begins with the act that inaugurates, at a particular moment, in a particular place, for a particular group, one particular democratic *method*. This act must seem to presuppose that there already is a group in a place that commences its democratic path at a certain moment. In fact, all these can only commence at the moment of the inaugural act itself. This may seem like an overly abstract formulation for what is involved in beginning a democracy, but only through this most general consideration does it become possible to find out what anyone means by democracy in the first place.

From the moment of its foundation the *way* of democracy, its method, becomes split between two aspects: the law, and the process of democratic decision-making. What is the law, in a democracy? At the most general level, it is the consequence of the recognition that there must be a way for determining when a democratic decision has been made, and a method for ensuring that general conditions are adequate for guaranteeing that a decision is in fact democratic. The law, then, is both the method for conducting elections and determining their outcomes, and the method for ensuring that the way in which people live makes possible proper participation in the political process. Generalized murder and mayhem are not just bad in themselves, but threaten the conditions under which democratic government is feasible. Law is nothing other than the means for ensuring the continuing possibility of pursuing the democratic way.

The process of making decisions in a democracy is of course also a matter of law, but it is not only that. Three forms of decision-making in Australia are immediately apparent. There is parliament, that debates and argues, in order finally to resolve to pass or defeat legislation put before it. There is the executive power of the Prime Minister and the Ministers. And there is a power to decide that is given to judges who, even though they must "follow" the law, nevertheless are those to whom is charged the responsibility of deciding what it is that the law *says*. These processes of decision-making each involve their own rules. But the difference between law and a process of making decisions is that the former is nothing other than the mechanics of rules to be obeyed, whereas the latter is supposed to be the framework through which legislators, the executive, and the judiciary are able to act and decide "freely."

But there is something peculiar about the parliamentary and the executive forms of making decisions. Parliament decides upon legislation, yet that legislation must then be signed into effect by the Governor-General. The Prime Minister and Ministers may make decisions in their own right, yet they do not become the Prime Minister and Ministers until they are declared to be so, again by the Governor-General. In both cases, the apparently sovereign decisions made by the representatives of the people are in some sense mediated by the figure of the head of state. Things need not have been arranged in this way, yet this arrangement nevertheless tells us something about the political system. If the will of the people is sovereign, then why is it that the representation of this will in the parliament and by the executive requires the official stamp of a non-elected head of state?

The answer to this question lies beyond the intricacies of constitutional history. The answer lies in the fact that the *act* that founds a democracy can be neither democratic nor legal. Democracy begins with a decision and a declaration: that there will be democracy. Without this decision and this declaration, democracy cannot commence. In other words, without the *stamp* of a quasi-official pronouncement that the decision to found a democracy *has been taken*, without the pronouncement that this is a real, that is, an *effective* decision, democracy cannot get underway. The truth of such a declaration is never certain at the moment of its pronouncement, and it remains in need of constant re-affirmation. This is not only a kind of anxiety contained within the structure of democracy, but a logical necessity.

The first person to declare a democracy, after all, is *not* elected, but has promised to preside over the first enactment of the democratic process, a promise, say, to make sure that there *is* an election and that it is conducted fairly and properly. The first government that is thus elected according to the newly inaugurated democratic procedure thus requires the official stamp that, yes, indeed, the election was fair and democratic, and that the government is the government. The first elected government needs the assurance that it is indeed the outcome of a democratic procedure. This assurance can never really be given, because the one who gives it must have the capacity to declare that the election was fair and democratic, although this person has not been placed into this position democratically. And this need for assurance, for a stamp, is carried along down the chain of governments. Beginning with an act of declaration, what we like to call "democracy" requires another declaration, another stamp of assurance, each time a "democratic" decision is undertaken.

The will of the people

In Australia, following the English model, the instituted method of democratic procedure is not only representative, but one in which the executive is decided from among the elected representatives that make up parliament. That this is so means another stamp is required, to declare that, among those elected, such and such a person has the support to command government. The Prime Minister, merely one elected member among a group of equal parliamentary members, thus relies upon continuing support from parliament in order to claim the democratic right to hold office. Where this support is lost, it becomes necessary to withdraw the stamp, and hence necessary either to form a government under a new Prime Minister, with a new stamp of authority, or else to determine that an election is required.

This distinguishes the Australian system from, for instance, the American system, where the executive is *not* made up of members of Congress, but as the outcome of a separate election. In the American system, then, the will of the people is split between two bodies, the

Congress and the president, which has led on occasion to complete paralysis of government. The only means for resolving this dual will into a single will is negotiation. This kind of negotiation is often praised by those who see it as a human "check" on the power of government, and hence as a protection of the people from the abuse of office by those in government. In Australia, such arguments are put by those who defend the role of the Senate as a house of review. The will of the people is split in Australia, as it is in the United States, between the House of Representatives and the Senate. The argument is frequently put that the Senate has been effective in tempering the excesses of governmental legislative zeal. This argument is conducted as though legislation is a rough-hewn piece of wood, and as though each passage through a house of parliament was like passing through a sanding tool, lopping off those branches on which the citizenry is likely to get caught, and leaving a finely polished piece of timber.

Yet there is no guarantee that a house of review will function in this way. There is no reason to believe that the balance of power in the Senate is more likely to fall into the hands of "moderate" parties than into the hands of "extreme" parties. It is entirely possible that the party controlling the balance of power will influence legislation toward dangerous possibilities. With only a small change in the way Australian history has unfolded, for instance, the One Nation party might now be controlling the balance of power in the Senate. The balance of power in Israeli parliaments has notoriously lain, from one government to the next, with very right wing religious parties that continuously drag government policy in a direction not necessarily favored by the public majority. It is a shortsighted defense of the role of the Senate in Australia that points only toward its most recent conduct.

Beyond the question of how a house of review is likely to behave is a more general question: how to understand what it means to split the will of the people into more than one representative body. Does the need for negotiation between houses, or between Congress and president, protect democracy from authoritarian rule? Is negotiation therefore a democratic principle? The answer is no. There is a fundamental difference between splitting the will of the people into two or more bodies, and in distributing it between several representatives of a single body. A chamber of parliament is nothing but a mechanism for resolving the will of the people into the possibility of decision. It works according to rules and with the goal of transparency.

What underlies the procedure of parliament is the thought that democracy means the possibility for the people to make decisions, a possibility that it intends to grant through the system of representation and debate. Negotiation *between* houses, or between Congress and president, is a fundamentally anti-democratic method, because negotiation works without rules and without transparency. Negotiation between bodies returns the procedure for making decisions to a private sphere, and reduces the accountability of the democratic representatives. The attractiveness of splitting the will of the people derives from the binary conception of government that sees it as essentially opposed to the will of the people. Yet the need for negotiation that this split entails also ensures that decisions lie at a *greater* distance from the will of the people, rather than nearer.

The best Australian example of the consequences of splitting the will of the people into two houses is not any "successful" negotiations that may have tempered the "extremes" of legislation (the Australian Democrats, for instance, point to the negotiations that led to the introduction of the GST, although these negotiations themselves will, among other things, most likely lead the Democrats to lose the balance of power they so cherish). The best example is still the dismissal of the Whitlam government in 1975, which was made possible by the paralysis between the government and the Senate. Paralysis means nothing other than a hostile body that, claiming a legitimate mandate from the people, refuses to negotiate. The dismissal was the singular moment in which the procedure of Australian democracy was tested at its limit. It is remarkable that argument about either the role of the Senate or the future of the head of state could be made without granting central importance to this event.

Understanding the events of 1975 means understanding the head of state, the Governor-General, as the one who grants the stamp of authority upon government and Prime Minister. What took place in 1975 was an intervention by the head of state to resolve the deadlock between two bodies claiming to hold a mandate from the people.

The means of this intervention was, firstly, to remove the stamp of authority from the Prime Minister; secondly, to declare the necessity for a new election; and thirdly, to grant a stamp of authority to a new Prime Minister as caretaker until the results of a new election could be determined. Each of these three interventions is possible because the head of state is the figure that grants or withholds the stamp of assurance about the legitimacy of a government or of a democratic decision.

Sovereign and automaton

What is odd about the head of state is the combination of absolute power and absolute powerlessness. On the one hand, it seems clear that the head of state is intended to be a functionary, a bureaucratic mechanism. The Governor-General declares the new Prime Minister, but in this matter can *only* choose that Member of Parliament who claims a majority of parliamentary support. The Governor-General signs legislation into existence but, again, this is a purely technical mechanism, and is not truly intended to mean that the *endorsement* of the head of state is a democratic requirement. The Governor-General is, it seems obvious to say, meant to be merely a rubber stamp and, perhaps, an ornament of the state, the perfect choice to officiate at bridge openings, etc. During the recent "scandal" leading to the downfall of Governor-General Hollingworth, those calling for his dismissal or resignation spoke at times about his diminished capacity for fulfilling his official duties. Yet, as long as his scissor-wielding hand was unimpaired, there should not have been any real detriment to this capacity, at least insofar as the technical requirements of the position are concerned.

On the other hand, however, the head of state in Australia continues to have the *potential* to wield enormous power. This power was exposed in 1975 and the shock of that event was the realization that, when Sir John Kerr decided to act, nothing could check his power. The Governor-General carries the capacity to undo the decision of the electorate, to unmake one Prime Minister and to make another, and there is no means of appealing against such decisions. It is a capacity that is explicitly non-justiciable. This extreme power in the hands of an appointed official seems utterly antithetical to the spirit of democracy.

Yet it is not. It is the head of state who ultimately protects democracy. Such a statement appears scandalous to those for whom the 1975 dismissal was the ultimate betrayal of the people's decision. And it is not intended here to defend Kerr. Yet what would Kerr's defense be, if not that the will of the people had been unacceptably stifled by the state of paralysis afflicting the houses of parliament, and thus that the interest of democracy itself demanded a circuit-breaker? Kerr's judgment regarding this question may have been woeful, if it was not merely a mask concealing his dislike of the government of the day. But the *argument* for the dismissal itself could hardly be conducted in terms other than as a defense of true democracy against the failure of its manifestation.

The head of state protects democracy because the way in which democracy begins – non-democratically, non-legally – means that there is never any certainty that we are yet *in* a democracy. Democracy begins with a risk; the risk is serious and it never goes away. The power of the head of state to dismiss a government is like an emergency escape hatch for democracy, in case of the worst. In case, that is, Hitler is "democratically" elected, which happened once. Hitler, it should not be forgotten, stated in his early days that he would be elected by democratic means, and that would be the end of elections. The power of the head of state is an attempt to cope with the uncertainty and the risk inherent in the commencement of democracy, the risk that this commencement was in error, or that subsequently something has gone seriously awry.

But that the head of state protects democracy does not imply that the actions of the head of state are themselves democratic. Dismissing a government, even in the name of democracy, is not itself democratic. And, within democracy, the head of state must not function as a king, even if in the end they share the same capacity to dissolve parliament. Providing an emergency escape hatch means entrusting it to somebody to deploy it correctly and at the right moment. But of course the risk that such a mechanism will be abused is a profound threat to democracy. The principle must be that it only be utilized at the time of greatest threat, when democracy hangs over a precipice, when true catastrophe looms. But in the end that still means: according to the judgment of the person entrusted with the power.

For the sake of democracy, the head of state must hold the power to undo the will of the people expressed according to the "system" of democracy. But, equally for the sake of democracy, there must be every deterrent to the deployment of this power, which ought truly to be held in reserve until the last possible moment. The head of state is thus monarch and automaton, sovereign and bureaucrat. Democracy is ultimately placed in the hands of the head of state, but with the presupposition that the head of state will not use this power until it is absolutely necessary.

There is something truly crazy about this system. But it is a craziness that emerges from the "logic" that means "democracy" never commences democratically. In whose hands should such a power be vested? It might be placed into the hands of the High Court, on the grounds that this returns the question of legitimate government to a legal basis. But to give judges the power to decide on governments in times of crisis makes them sovereign. Democracy is then only an epiphenomenon within the functioning of law. In 2000, for instance, we witnessed the spectacle of the Supreme Court being asked to adjudicate the Florida election, and hence being asked to choose the next president of the United States of America. This could only occur because in America there is no separate head of state whose actions are, according to juridical discourse, "non-justiciable," not available for determination by a court. In the end, that election was determined by the Florida legislature, an outcome that is just as peculiar, since the "whole" is then determined by one of its "parts," so to speak. The point is that it is just as skewed for one legislative body to determine the outcome of an election as it is for a court to determine that outcome. In both cases, the will of the people is no longer the determinant in the last instance.

The head of state is thus the third "figure" of democracy, along-side the will of the people, and the autonomous will of "the law." This figure stands between the other two, without independent authority yet inaccessible to either of the contending forces. The head of state is suspended between the system that represents the will of the people and the legal system, as a kind of pivot. It is both a religious and a poetic figure, but of a religion and poetry, ideally, of democracy itself. The head of state should be neither figurehead for nor reflection of the people. Rather, the head of state is both above and below the people. The head of state is above the people in embodying the determinant in the last instance. As such, it is a position that represents democracy itself, potentially in opposition to its electoral manifestation. Yet the head of state is below the people in that, in all ordinary, everyday functioning, the head of state has no "right" to act other than according to the wishes of the electorate and the legislature. Thus the Prime Minister has the right (through a request put to the monarch) to appoint or dismiss the Governor-General at will.

The ideal head of state, then, is one for whom there is *no* mandate, rather than the mandate of the people. Australia's current constitutional arrangement displays this in a singular way. The authority of the head of state is removed, as it were, from both ends. On the one side, the Governor-General, appointed at the whim of the Prime Minister, has no mandate from the people. On the other side, as the *representative* of the monarch, the Governor-General does not have a mandate even to act according to his or her own conscience. More specifically, the conscience of the Governor-General is related to his or her decisions only insofar as this relates to their responsibility *to the monarch*. The peculiar thing about the dismissal of 1975 was that the Governor-General may have claimed to have been acting out of concern for the people, on the grounds that the will of the people had been stymied by governmental paralysis. What *actually* renders the decision of Sir John Kerr doubtful was not the relation of his actions to the people, but his failure to consult the Queen, thus failing properly to fulfil his role as the monarch's representative.

Were the Governor-General to become a President, then, even if everything else should remain the same, this one plank on which to argue against the actions of future Kerrs would have been removed. This is not to say that retaining a head of state as merely the representative of an offshore monarch is any kind of *guarantee* that no repetition of 1975 is possible. The very position is the embodiment of the impossibility of guarantees at all. Yet there is something supremely delicate about the position of head of state as impossibly balanced between the people and the law. There is something incredibly delicate as well about the way in which the mandate of the head of state to act is withdrawn both from below (the head of state is not the people's politician), and from above (the head of state is neither the monarch nor the representative of God on earth).

The head of state must not act, according to such an arrangement, unless it is absolutely necessary. This necessity is dictated neither from God nor from conscience, but from the necessity of democracy itself, a thought of democracy *beyond* the will of the people insofar as it has until the present been manifested. Such an argument for the current constitutional arrangement risks, admittedly, seeming pedantic or ethereal. Yet if one accepts, as both the monarchists and republicans do, that the head of state is a necessary position, then what becomes important is how well this risky and delicate position can be maintained in its state of impossible suspension.

Dangerous supplements

What is intended by the claim that the head of state is both a religious and poetic figure has not yet been made sufficiently clear. That the head of state is a religious figure does not mean that the position embodies a reference to God, or derives its authority from the figure of God. Australia's current constitutional arrangements do not "prove themselves" through the figure of Governor-General to be founded in a monotheological conception of the relation of humanity to divinity. And yet, as standing above the people, as the embodiment of decision in the last instance, as representative of a sovereign power, the head of state does reflect a theological conception of the place of humanity. But the god in question here is the god of democracy itself. The higher power, the ultimate ground, beyond the people, beyond the conscience even of the head of state, is the thought of democracy. The head of state can act legitimately only when a gap opens between the expression of the will of the people and democracy "itself," whatever that might mean.

The obscurity of this thought, the obscurity of democracy "itself," contains the clue to the meaning of the thought that the head of state is a "poetic" figure. And this clue becomes manifest in the fact that, alongside the campaign and the referendum concerning the republic, there was another campaign and referendum. This second referendum concerned the question of whether a preamble should be added to the Australian Constitution. This additional campaign had its own peculiar narrative, involving drafts and counter-drafts, and was probably doomed even before the question of the republic. But it had its own curious charm, as well. And much of this charm came from the fact that a preamble is a *text*, with *words*, which meant that it was debated, at least to some degree, in terms of content rather than merely form.

The pros and cons of a preamble, or of any particular preamble, will not be discussed here. The short answer must be: it depends. It is neither necessarily the case that a preamble is dangerous, nor that it is beneficial. What made the debate about a preamble strangely interesting was the ambiguity about whether the preamble *made any difference* in law. Is a preamble a declaration of new principles, that will determine the interpretation of the Constitution, and hence that may constrain future legislators? Or is it only an ornament that decorates the Constitution, a declaration of spirit with no juridical effect? In which case, the debate about a preamble is even more trivial than the debate about the title of the head of state.

The truth of the matter, insofar as it exists at all, seems to lie somewhere between these two possibilities. A preamble, perhaps, does not *determine* the possibility or impossibility of new laws, but in some vague way functions as a beacon by which judges and legislators may be guided away from dangerous waters and towards proper paths. The preamble is then more than an ornament but less than a set of new articles to the Constitution. It is a strange kind of supplement to the body of the Constitution, a supplementarity that risks being only onanistic, a declaration of good will and good intentions without any force. It is, at best, a weapon in the arsenal of judges with which they can bolster decisions about constitutional interpretation. A preamble is something like a prayer.

It is more than an accident that the question of the republic was tied to the question of the preamble. In both cases what is at stake is the "legitimacy" of the Constitution, that is, the legitimacy of what we call democracy in Australia. And in both cases, the "guarantee" of this legitimacy is characterized by an ambiguity concerning its *effect*. Both the preamble and the head of state are intended somehow to add some weight, to *increase* legitimacy, to ensure that "democracy" really is democratic, but in both cases it is far from clear what *difference* they are supposed to make. Thus the fact that these "issues" have arisen recently reflects two things: firstly, an *insecurity* about the legitimacy of Australian sovereignty, and a corresponding need to supplement the constitutional system, to *boost* its legitimacy. The questions concerning the preamble and the head of state reflect this sense of anxiety, and this need to reinforce the sense that our democratic way is indeed *proper*.

But at the same time these questions reflect an anxiety that, in the haste to supplement the Constitution and the constitutional system, there lies a risk. And that is the risk that we lack the wisdom and the foresight to *achieve* the desired reinforcement. These supplements may in fact be dangerous. Hence there is a constantly repeated equivocation about whether these supplements make a difference, whether *changes* are being proposed, or whether in fact everything will remain the same. There is, then, a counterbalance to the need to reinforce the sense of the legitimacy of the Constitution. And that is the wish to ensure that, if there is change, it should be little more than cosmetic, little more than a matter of public relations. There is a lack of confidence, probably justified, that we are in a position to know what changes really are for the better. This lack of confidence comes in spite of the certainty that the Constitution is flawed.

Theologico-poetic sovereignty

To reconstruct the tale of the lead-up to the referendum on the preamble would be tedious, with the many proposals and counterproposals overlapping each other to the point of virtual indistinction. A hermeneutic account of what was at stake with each variation would be even more interminable. Rather, a brief examination of one newspaper article about one brief phase of this process will suffice. On 4 March 1999, on the front page of the Melbourne *Age*, an article occupying center stage was headed "Poet is ready to preambulate." In order to place the importance of this article within the context of serious global affairs at the time, it should be pointed out that it was placed immediately above another article with the heading, "Lewinsky tells: My soulmate."

Above the headline and dominating the article is a large photograph of the Australian poet Les Murray against a rust colored garage door holding an akubra hat. Under the photograph is the following caption:

> "God's gotta be in there (in the preamble)," says Les Murray on the eve of his meeting with John Howard.

Before the article even begins, therefore, the preamble has been associated with the poetic and the theological. What is more, the *figure* of the poet has already been associated with, yet distanced from, the figure of the politician. The poet is to the politician what the head priest used to be to the monarch who rules with divine sanction: the figure who assures the divinity – the legitimacy – of the rule, by virtue of being in communication *with* the divine. And if the head priest depends for his life on communicating to the subjects that the monarch's rule is divine, he must also communicate to that monarch that he is the proper voice of divine authority: God's gotta be in there. Hence the head priest is both subordinate to the monarch yet transcends earthly power, such that the monarch must at least *apparently* be dependent upon the priest.

And thus the article, by Caroline Overington, begins.

> When Australia's unofficial poet laureate, the masterful Les Murray, meets the Prime Minister, John Howard, to discuss the new preamble to the Constitution today . . .

This portion of an opening sentence already tells us everything we need to know about the situation being manufactured. The bare facts are that at the beginning of the process leading to a referendum on the preamble, the Prime Minister determined that he required the assistance of a specialist to assist with its formulation. The specialist should not, must not, be a constitutional scholar or lawyer, because the preamble is not law. The preamble exceeds ordinary law, inhabiting a more ethereal realm. It is, perhaps, a guide to the law, both to the interpretation of existing law and to the framing of new law.

Furthermore, the preamble transforms the Constitution itself, pushing it in the direction of becoming a document, or a method, of civic education. The preamble is a miniaturized narrative of the "we" who founded Australia, and the "we" who will continue the narrative *of* Australia. The preamble makes the Constitution into the means for transmitting from one generation to the next that there is a "we" who came together, legitimately founded a democracy, and entrusted to future generations the task of continuing what was then begun. For that, neither a lawyer nor a historian is adequate: a poet is needed.

Not only a poet but a poet laureate, that is, the poet *of* the nation. The double genitive should be audible here. The poet laureate is the one who, through poetry, does more than commentate on or chronicle the nation, but guides it. This guidance is more than just advice; it is more like authorizing or authoring the destiny of the nation, contributing to its self-invention. The poet adds the laurel to the crown, and thus is needed by the Prime Minister. Every proper nation requires its poet laureate. Yet is Australia a proper nation? Is any nation proper? The relative youth of the Australian nation means there is insecurity about the validity of any national poet, which is why he remains, at all times, *unofficial.* "When Australia's unofficial poet laureate . . ."

There is a place, Australia: it exists. If there is a place, it needs its proper poet. Its sovereign needs the supplement of a laurel. But doubt remains. Are we a nation? Have we a sovereign? Do we believe in a poet who can crown that sovereign, the sovereignty of our Constitution? The poet remains unofficial. Yet, remaining unofficial, the article is saying, the poet, like the nation, nevertheless does, in fact, exist. And he does so (the sentence is gaining confidence here) *masterfully.* Our poet laureate is unofficial yet masterful, and his remaining unofficial is in fact *evidence* of his mastery. Not requiring the stamp of officialdom, the poet's mastery of language is a mastery that transcends the mastery of legal language. Thus, in the body of the article, Murray is quoted as saying that being called in by the Prime Minister to write a draft preamble was not an honor but merely a job. Concerning politics, he adds, mock naïvely: "Most of it goes over my head."

The poet is beyond the political, and hence in contact with the divine, even if this contact is itself unofficial and not too priestly. The article says:

> One thing is certain: if the Prime Minister takes Murray's advice, the preamble will begin with the words "Under God . . ." (Murray is a convert to Roman Catholicism, "the full disaster").

A preamble is to the Constitution and the nation as a nice rug is to an apartment: it really ties the room together. Murray describes this tie as not a matter of being legally bound, but of being bound in sentiment. And, still, however unofficially, what ties the tie is the reference to the divine: God's gotta be in there.

Les Murray had already drafted a preamble, included in the *Age* article, for her sister publication, the *Sydney Morning Herald*. The poet's preamble consisted of three sentences. The first, beginning "Under God . . . ," is a declaration that Australia has been constituted (as a republic) through the sovereignty of all its citizens. It is, therefore, a repetition of the first declarative act rather than a statement of historical fact. It is stating more than that an originary act occurred that founded Australia. It is stating that Australia continues to be because it continues to be constituted through the continuing sovereignty of its citizens. The second sentence is a declaration of the borders of the nation (an island continent plus certain other smaller bits), as well as an "acknowledgment" that there were prior inhabitants.

The final sentence is surprising, and challenging to comprehension: "Government in Australia exists to serve and protect all citizens in an equal dignity which may never be infringed by fashion or ideology, nor invoked against achievement." What is the poet trying to communicate here? Government has a purpose: to serve and protect all citizens in an equal dignity. If there is no mention of democracy in this preamble, there is at least the recognition that government ought not be the master of its citizens. But, of all the threats to the service and protection offered by government, it is odd that those mentioned in the preamble should be fashion and ideology. These are the enemies of good government, according to the poet, those enemies so threatening they must be warned against in the preamble. If we wish to see his words in a favorable light, we might say that we are being warned about the dangers of dogmatism and fanaticism. The poet speaks the common sense voice of Australia in its suspicion of politics. More abstractly, it is the threat posed by the distortion of language. This distortion occurs through the superficiality of the most current ideas, and the false certainty of the ideologue.

But it is difficult not to hear this as the voice of the poet's fear of or contempt for critics. The poet, especially the poet laureate, especially the religious poet laureate, wishes his poetry to do more than conform to the fashions and ideologies of his time, which can only be the earthly and material virtues of a decadent culture. And this feeling is only reinforced by the end of the sentence, which proclaims the importance of recognizing *achievement* (that is, those who achieve), even (so it seems) at the expense of serving and protecting the equal dignity of all. At the very least, it is impossible not to hear this sentence as a critique of what is fashionably and ideologically (that is, politically) referred to as "the chattering classes".

Of course, this draft of a possible preamble submitted to a Fairfax publication had no chance of being adopted by official politics, even by those politicians who might be sympathetic to the idea of being bound by its sentiments. The draft was, if anything, too "political" for the politicians, and not "poetic" enough. Eventually the politicians would trust *themselves* to add the poetry and remove the politics from the preamble. And what would guide them in such an exercise was the people's will, even if the referendum was doomed. Like the question of the head of state, the overriding principle was minimalism, not to offend the distrust and the aesthetics of the electorate. Thus "more poetic" means more predictable, more idyllic, less quirky, less "unofficial." Murray failed because he wasn't bureaucratic enough, because he did not write enough like an automaton, and because on the contrary he wrote more like somebody wishing to claim a mandate, the mandate of the poetic achiever.

In the end, the only viable option would be a preamble that sounded how a preamble "should" sound: virtuous and hollow. In this it reflected the kinds of (non-)arguments put forward for a republic. The great political event of the end of the first century of the Commonwealth of Australia was, decidedly, appropriately, and thankfully, a complete fizzer. Both referenda failed badly. Perhaps the phoenix will rise again. Perhaps when it does so, it will prove an event of significance, punctuating time's march in the experience of Australians. No such significance can be attributed to the efforts of the republican movement at the end of the twentieth century. But when this first effort has long been forgotten by those who lived to experience it, it is sure to achieve an afterlife. Like an undead zombie in the textbooks of future generations of Australian school students, it will march on as yet another dramatic narrative in the great arc of Australian history.

Chapter 5

Border Protection and Alien Friends

It is idle to urge that, because this ship can go anywhere the captain likes to take it, and because the applicant is free to go wherever the ship goes, that he is not imprisoned. What answer is that to this application? Compelling him to stay on board the ship is exactly what the applicant complains of as an illegal restraint upon his liberty.

Justice Victor Windeyer[1]

If democracy means that one particular group of individuals gives itself the right to decide on the way and the rules by which it lives, then what has already been determined is that there is a border. Democracy means democracy for those within the border, to the exclusion of those lying beyond the border. To extend the vote to all those outside our border, for instance, would in effect give *them* control over *us*, thereby extinguishing democracy. More generally, if democracy depends upon the existence of a group, of the integrity of that group, then from the moment the border is instituted, those within its borders must be able to decide when and how the border may be crossed. Border control and border protection are not a threat to democracy, then, but its very precondition. At least, that is, to democracy insofar as it has been understood in our time. If a democracy loses the capacity to control and to protect its borders, the capacity for remaining democratic is undermined.

This does not mean borders must never be crossed, that strangers and aliens must never be admitted, either as visitors or as fully constituted members. The crossing of borders is not in itself a threat to democracy, and those nations that call themselves democracies have always permitted such crossings. But they have done so, always, on their own terms, and have reserved the right to open or close borders, to some or to all, according to decisions of their own making. What these terms and decisions are may be debated within the borders of the group, but it is only those within the borders who have a say in such a debate. This is the principle repeatedly stated by Australian Prime Minister John Howard during the 2001 Australian federal election campaign: "We will decide who comes to this country and the circumstances in which they come."

What argument could be advanced against such a claim? Everything depends upon the decision that there is a "we." "We will decide . . ." As soon as the "we" is treated as real, as *true*, as soon as it is admitted that "we Australians" exist, then democratic principle demands that we retain the right to decide on our border regime. If Australia has the right to exist, if we Australians have the right to govern ourselves, then by definition we have the right to control and protect our borders. Who could usurp such a right? Without borders, without the borders that define who we are, we have as little ability to decide to "let them in" as we do to "keep them out."

The only way to properly argue against the proposition that we will decide who comes to this country and the circumstances in which they come, is to argue against the "we" itself. If there is no "us" separate from "them," that is, if "we" aren't separated from them by a border, then we lose the right to control and protect our borders. If we argue, for instance, that there is a greater "we," "we humanity," say, that overrides our self-determination as Australians, then perhaps we have obligations that derive from this membership in a greater community. Or perhaps the recognition that all of us are part of one group, humanity, demands that "we," "we Australians," decide one way rather than another about "our" local borders, for the good of the greater "us." This is the argument that the sovereignty of human rights is greater than the sovereignty of local democracy, or at least that the latter is modified by the former.

Democracies are perfectly able to assume obligations in relation to the treatment of aliens and strangers, but they always do so *by choice*, by agreeing to an international convention, say. Even when agreeing to a convention, however, even when ratifying it, the convention still does not have the legal force of legislation. When judges interpret the law, they must do so *first of all* by relying on the legislation of parliament, and only secondarily by taking into account treaties and conventions that have been signed or ratified by government or parliament. And if judges must turn to legislation first, this is according to the properly democratic principle that those laws decided and determined by the people are those laws that must be granted the greatest weight in judicial reasoning.

Nevertheless, when arguing against particular methods of border protection and border control, the most common resort is to the sense that there is an obligation to those lying beyond our borders, or those who cross into our territory. Such arguments are usually presented as the contest between the "universalism" of human rights and the "particular" decisions of local legislatures. The argument essentially consists of the exhortation to remember that "they are people too." Beyond our local group there is the universal group to which we all belong.

Of course, this is obviously not really "universalism." In virtue of remaining a *group*, even the group "humanity" is still particular. There is still a decision involved, about the borders of the group. It is not only a matter of differentiating first of all between "humanity" and the *other* "animals." The Nazis might claim a kind of universalism that makes the "master race" into the *true* humanity, and all those other people into merely animals or some kind of degenerated humanity. If this strikes our ear as absurd, this is because of the tendency to see the Nazis as making an error of fact: the Jews *are*, truly, biologically, objectively, people too. But is it so clear that our best choice is to respond to their "biologism" with our own, with the assertion that, truly, biologically, objectively, there is such a thing as humanity that has greater limits than they, the Nazis, will admit? The assumption that *we* know who the animals are is always risky.

To counter the thought of a master race with a biological argument is to rely upon a scientific definition of the human. Despite the fondness of biologists for categorization, they resist entering such definitional debates. The same is true for medical science. Whether life begins at conception, at birth, at some point between, or at some later date, is a question about the borders of humanity. These are temporal borders but they become *political* questions, a matter of deciding who is a person, who counts as a who. Those who view abortion as murder are simply operating under a wide definition of the borders of humanity. No decision about such borders can be dictated scientifically. But if not scientifically, what authority can compel us one way or another?

There is a contest, then, between those who extol the principle of universal humanity and those who assert the pre-eminence of the counterprinciple of the sovereignty of national borders. But this is not truly a contest between universalism and nationalism, particularism, or localism. It is not a contest between those who defend a world of borders, and those who argue for a planet *sans frontières*. Rather, it is always and necessarily a question of *which* borders, where to draw them, how widely or narrowly, how generously or protectively. And the means by which to do so.

Capital and citizenship

Our planet has never been more criss-crossed with borders, and those borders have never been the focus of greater political attention. The walled cities of the past were less a matter of groupings determined politically, less about citizenship, than they were about specifically military protection, about protection in the event of *attack*. Keeping people in and keeping them out, controlling their movements, was really only important in terms of the possibility of *war*. These walled cities succumbed to the essentially economic pressures of expansion, and the fall of these walls did not occasion any great fear that the inhabitants would lose their "identity."

For our contemporary economico-technical planetary system, borders are both more concrete and more porous than ever before. And this distinction between the concrete and the porous conforms to the distinction between citizenship and capital. Capital flies across the globe with ever decreasing restraint. The borders that define citizenship, however, have become a political question of increasing urgency in many states. At least in the West. What is at stake between the variously concrete and porous borders is economic. "Immigration" and "border protection" become political questions most commonly when the citizens of impoverished states migrate to more wealthy states. Americans wishing to migrate is not a burning political issue in Haiti. Borders aren't to keep out refugees; they are to keep out the wretched poor. On the other hand, the right of the capitalist to trade freely across the globe continues to grow. We are all one people, insofar as we have the capacity to *invest*. And, while *capital* moves freely, the interests of capital may equally be served by constraining the movement of *labor* within those borders.

It is not a matter of "explaining" that border protection is a political issue because it serves the interests of capital to control labor. The relation between capitalism and political culture is not so direct as to make the latter into *simply* the projection of the requirements of the former. Nevertheless, it is equally obvious that economics plays a large part in the emergence of the issue of border protection. The fear of invasion is, amongst other things, most certainly a fear of an invasion of labor, the fear that "they" will "steal" "our" jobs. Such fears fuel the concern with border protection, and such concerns serve the interests of capital. Nevertheless, a strange irony is at work, at least in a country such as Australia, because the fear that "their" migration will lead to "our" unemployment flies in the face of a virtual consensus of economic opinion that population growth will lead to economic growth. Of course, economic growth is not necessarily the same thing as employment growth. That an economy can grow while unemployment remains high may not be the result of immigration. Yet the fear of unemployment contributes to resentment against migrant laborers. And the fear itself may well lie in a justifiable perception of "our" economic future.

Bipartisanship and populism

The fear of immigration has a long history in Australia, and has usually taken the form of a fear of racial contamination, of being overwhelmed by aliens. This fear, and its political expression, has transcended party politics, being at least as prominent in the Labor tradition as the conservative. It is remarkable that a nation founded so recently and entirely by migrants could so clearly manifest this fear throughout its short history. Perhaps the White Australia policy was a reflection of a need to assert that there indeed *is* a nation called Australia, that there really *is* "a people" capable of attaining nationhood, rather than simply the remnants of a penal colony.

Perhaps such racial fears are testament to the fragility of the sense of actually constituting a "we," rather than to its strength.

Whatever the explanation, politicians within the borders of Australia have usually been able to count upon a favorable response to airing "concerns" about migration. Nevertheless, as everyone also knows, the migration in question has almost always been not only lawful, but governmentally *planned*. For many decades now, migration to Australia has been planned for and organized by governments on economic grounds. But the sense that migration is economically necessary has never interfered with the capacity for it to occasion the raising of grave fears and doubts about its consequences, thus leading to a cheerfully self-perpetuating circle.

Most politicians are opportunists, frequently cynical and usually ambitious. Politicians from all sides decide strategically which issues to adopt and which to avoid. At the same time, however, politicians almost always manage to perceive themselves as virtuous, acting for the benefit of the community. For this reason, the mind of the politician frequently holds antithetical notions in relation to immigration: on the one hand, the prudent awareness that migration is economically beneficial; on the other hand, the cunning awareness that the popular fear of immigration provides an opportunity for political advancement. But there is *also* the awareness that what can be exploited by one side of politics can as easily be exploited by the other. And hence if both sides take the opportunistic choice, there is a risk of raising the stakes in a political game to an unacceptably high level. Were that allowed to occur, the capacity to pursue a necessary policy of economic immigration would be threatened. The unease this thought produced resulted in what was called, in the Australian context, the "bipartisan" approach to immigration.

Bipartisanship was, essentially, an agreement between opposing sides of politics. It was an agreement *not* to speak publicly about immigration as though it were an issue about which one had to take sides. The question of capital punishment has received the same bipartisan treatment for a long time in Australian political culture. This does not mean that oppositions conspire with governments to keep secrets about immigration policy from the electorates they serve. Policies, decisions, figures, statistics, are all publicly available to those who seek them out. But there is public and there is public. The bipartisan approach to immigration policy means an agreement that those major avenues of communication, that is, the "media," will not be "used" by one political side or the other to "exploit" immigration by "inflaming" the public.

The way politicians defend this bipartisan policy *to themselves* is by disdain for what is called "populism." "Mainstream" politicians, then, disdain policies on the grounds that they may be popular. The term "populism" derives from the Populist Party, founded in 1892 in the United States by farmers unhappy with the way they were being served by the political process. One of their major concerns was the consequences upon themselves of the advancing world market, and among their policies was control or outright governmental ownership of public goods such as railroad and telegraph companies. The Populists were a threat to the southern Democrats, and thus the target of concerted attack, in a manner similar to that suffered more recently by presidential candidate Ralph Nader. It would be possible to write a history of the declining fortunes of the word "populism." Essentially, populism comes to mean the political strategy of "appealing to rednecks." Whether the issue is immigration or capital punishment, the bipartisan rejection of populist strategy means a disdain for what is popular, and the sense that the political professional is more civilized, more rational, less ignorant and more sensible than the community he or she intends to represent.

If the bipartisan approach to immigration is preferable to the White Australia policy that preceded it, what must also be acknowledged is that bipartisanship itself bore a cost and constituted a risk. The *cost* was to that political process popularly referred to as democracy. If a large group of people hold an issue to be important, and if the representatives of that group maintain an artificial silence about that issue, then, no matter how "irrational" the issue may be, that group justifiably feels unrepresented. And that lack of representation translates into a feeling of detachment from the "democratic process." The political process is then perceived as a technocratic and élitist system removed from anything truly democratic. And the *risk* to those who adopt such a bipartisan approach is that other opportunists will emerge to fill the vacuum of resentment left by this distance between the political system and the concerns of the electorate.

One Nation

Many would say that it was John Howard in the 1980s who broke the covenant of bipartisanship surrounding immigration policy in Australia, when he questioned the racial balance of immigrants. He stuck his toe in the water and, finding the temperature unacceptably high, withdrew it, hoping the sting he received would not be a lasting burn. One would have to say he appears unscarred, yet race has been a taboo topic ever since. What should not be forgotten is that it was during the same period that the ALP first decided the best accommodation for what were then called "boat people" was in detention centres.

But it was only with the election of the independent Pauline Hanson to the federal House of Representatives that a politician emerged prepared to seize the opportunity presented to her by the fact of bipartisanship. To the extent that such bipartisanship was maintained, she could justify her claim to be giving voice to the voiceless. Her positions on trade tariffs and on privatization made her into a true inheritor of the populist tradition of 1892. But it was her preparedness to raise immigration as a political issue that turned her into a potentially powerful force in the Australian political landscape.

What is less frequently observed, however, is that the threat was not equal on both sides of the House. Depending upon how much support One Nation could eventually muster, it may one day have been a threat to Labor. What was most immediately and obviously the case was that One Nation threatened to split the conservative vote, handing government to the ALP. Indubitably some in the ALP felt that One Nation represented an overall threat to Australian political culture. But it is just as certain that the growth of One Nation served the *immediate* political interests of the ALP.

With this in mind one can begin to understand the rhetoric from the ALP about One Nation. There was calculation behind this rhetoric, even if not everyone was equally conscious of what was being calculated. When the ALP claimed that One Nation was dividing Australia, the ALP was trying to divide the country. Their strategy was to paint the Coalition into a corner. By turning Pauline Hanson into as large a bogeyman as possible, Howard would be faced with an impossible choice. The vehicle for this strategy was the demand that the Liberals and Nationals state publicly and definitively whether they would preference One Nation last.

Howard must condemn Hanson as Hitler-in-waiting, and therefore preference One Nation last, the ALP cried. Thus many of those who identified with Hanson as the victimized voice of the silent majority would hopefully preference away from the Coalition. Alternatively, if the Coalition tried to keep the Hansonites on side by directing preferences *to* One Nation, they risked losing the support of the socially liberal, mostly urban Liberals, the "civilized" conservative voters. In other words, the ALP strategy was essentially a *dare*. Howard must come out and support the populism of Hanson, or simply give up that portion of the conservative vote the National Party traditionally mops up. And thus, in practice, One Nation was an issue of genuine conscience for the Coalition far more than it ever was for the ALP. More than one member of the National Party was driven to tears by the question of whether to preference for or against their new enemy. It was not only One Nation but also the ALP that was responsible for these tears.

The problem with painting someone into a corner is that eventually they realize that the only way out is straight ahead. The ALP knew that the Coalition could not win either way on the preferences question, but they failed sufficiently to consider how Howard might fight back. The ALP dare was a political gamble, and not only a strategic electoral gamble, but a gamble with the future of Australian politics. Most politicians are opportunists, as has been stated. Hanson is an opportunist. Howard is an opportunist. But the Coalition would have happily agreed to a bipartisan policy of ignoring Hanson and her ragtag party, of denying her "oxygen" and eventually condemning her to the political insignificance of the League of Rights. But the opportunism and the desperation of the ALP meant they preferred to gamble. To that extent, it was neither the outsider Hanson nor the Coalition that ended the bipartisan policy on immigration. It was the Australian Labor Party.

The Coalition had two strategies for dealing with One Nation. One was to discredit the party and its leader in the eyes of the public. The extent to which this strategy was pursued has only recently become visible, with the revelations about Tony Abbott's role in Hanson's legal problems. The other strategy by which the Coalition defended itself against an oxygenated One Nation was to take the dare. If you dare me to descend to populism, Howard said as the *Tampa* pulled into view, I hereby accept. And thus the ALP, with their attempt to win government by dividing the conservative vote, succeeded only in condemning themselves to an electoral catastrophe, and in dividing themselves and their supporters into those who could forgive Kim Beazley's disastrous opportunism, and those who could not.

Victory on the wine dark sea

Borders work differently at sea. A border on land is a means of confinement, or at least of regulating passage. The sea itself, divided by convention into various oceans, is nevertheless without borders, the very figure of undivided immensity. *At* sea, every vessel is its own bordered space. Alone on the open sea, mariners must rely upon one another, because the water line is a border to an abyss. From the *Odyssey* onward, a boat that traverses the vast expanse of ocean has been the very metaphor for the sovereign existence of the individual contending for survival against the greater might of nature. If modern day container ships seem part of a planetary transportation system that has conquered the borders of space and time, nevertheless every seaman is trained to understand the danger that the sea poses to those who venture upon it. That anyone could become its victim is the basis for the ancient principle, universally held, that a vessel in distress must always be attended to by any ship that can reach it. In those exceptional circumstances, where it is a matter of survival, there are no nations at sea. Anyone may enter my vessel, if their only alternative is to be cast into the dark and welcoming ocean.

The *Tampa* event was a spectacular demonstration of the way in which politicians will play with the lives of others to advance their own ambitions. This is surprising only to those who have failed to grasp that war is frequently an even more spectacular demonstration of the same phenomenon. But it was also an event in which the logic of borders at sea was forced into a confrontation with the logic of land borders. The standoff between Captain Arne Rinnan of the *Tampa* and the Australian government was a clash between two versions of the meaning of borders. For Rinnan, when on 26 August 2001 the fishing vessel *Palapa* sent a mayday, the ancient obligation to assist those in distress, whoever they may be and at whatever cost, came into force.

But when he then steered the 433 rescuees into Australian waters, the government chose to assert what would be referred to in subsequent court proceedings as an "ancient prerogative." What was thereby invoked was the prerogative of the executive in a sovereign, bordered state to decide whether to accept or repel aliens, either enemy or friend. The question to be settled, then, was between a mariner's obligation and a sovereign's prerogative, both with ancient roots. In a legal and in an extralegal sense, what was being put into question by this event was the border between land and sea itself.

This may sound grandiose, lending an almost mythological significance to what was *really* a contest between a government and its opposition during an election campaign. It was a battle carried out not in courtrooms or between philosophies, but on television and talkback radio. It was the first battle that resulted from the end of a bipartisan immigration policy, a policy that the government chose to end but, as has been argued, for which the ALP also bears grave responsibility. And it was a battle the Prime Minister won as comprehensively as he could have imagined, utterly trumping Beazley's Opposition.

Pauline Hanson was right to say the Coalition had "picked up" the policies and themes of One Nation. But that it did so was less the result of pressure from Hanson than it was due to the incessant challenge from Labor to take a stand in relation to One Nation. When the moment of truth arrived, when Howard accepted the challenge and the opportunity afforded by the *Tampa*, the utter weakness of the Labor strategy was immediately exposed. Already by 29 August, three days after the *Palapa* sent its mayday, Labor's "principled" stand against Hansonism had sunk with the *Palapa* to the bottom of an ignoble abyss. This, and the subsequent electoral fate of the ALP, were decisively signaled when the leader of the opposition stood in parliament to offer his complete capitulation:

> In these circumstances, this country and this parliament do not need a carping Opposition; what they actually need is an Opposition that understands the difficult circumstances in which the government finds itself, and to the very best of my ability I will ensure that that situation prevails.[2]

Nevertheless, if the real battle was between political parties fighting for no better reason than to achieve victory, it was still also the case that for several weeks there were two arenas of contest. One arena was aboard the *Tampa*, lying with its 433 rescuees just off the Australian territory of Christmas Island. And the other arena was the Australian Federal Court, where the battle was conducted between Eric Vadarlis and the Victorian Council for Civil Liberties on the one hand, and the Minister for Immigration and Multicultural Affairs, Philip Ruddock, on the other hand. A physical, or geographic arena, then, and an arena of contested argument. The way in which one side would eventually triumph could not be attributed solely either to the material arena off Christmas Island, nor to the ideal arena of Federal Court. Only by waging its war simultaneously in both fields was the government able to assert its sovereign prerogative to protect its borders over the obligation of the Captain to safely disembark his rescuees. This is the truth amply demonstrated in the remarkable account of those cynical campaign days by David Marr and Marian Wilkinson, *Dark Victory*.

The case

The first court proceedings were held between 2 and 5 September before Justice Anthony North. During that period the *pro bono* lawyers who brought the case agreed to allow the government to transfer the rescuees from the *Tampa* to the troopship *Manoora*. This transfer was portrayed by the government as necessary on humanitarian grounds, and as proof of its compassion. The lawyers acting to compel the government to accept the rescuees agreed to the transfer to the *Manoora* for two reasons: because the government threatened publicly to blame these lawyers for any suffering of those forced to remain on the *Tampa*; and because the government threatened to seek from these lawyers the full cost of the entire operation surrounding the affair should it win the case.[3] However understandable these reasons were, it was at the moment that such an agreement was reached that the fate of those 433 rescuees was decided.

Justice North's decision was delivered on 11 September 2001. Perhaps one reason for the difference in outcomes between this decision and the decision of the justices upon appeal is the subsequent impact of the other event of that day. It is not a matter of arguing that judges were influenced by a political climate, or indeed a climate of shock. Nevertheless, after 11 September certain kinds of argument and certain ways of perceiving situations – friends and enemies, of protection and prerogatives – had greater weight than they did on 10 September. When Justice North formulated his decision and its reasons, the necessity of the sovereign right to repel aliens at will had not the significance it came to have by the time of the appeal.

Justice North agreed with the lawyers who brought the case that the rescuees were effectively and completely detained by the government. The manner in which the government regulated the movement of the rescuees, and the manner in which it controlled the access of others *to* the rescuees, amounted to an enforced border against movement and communication. Having been unable to prevent the *Tampa* from crossing the invisible border of Australian territorial waters, the government had unlawfully contained those aboard the *Tampa*. The government had done so, not only to prevent them from setting foot on land, but to prevent them from communicating with anyone through whom they could claim asylum. The judge thereby accepted the applicability of *habeas corpus*, ordering the release of the rescuees. But as they were now aboard the *Manoora*, which had departed Australian territory, this order took the form of an order not only to release those persons rescued at sea by the *Tampa*, but to "bring those persons ashore to a place on the mainland of Australia."[4]

The appeal

This victory was shortlived. The appeal was heard on 13 September before Chief Justice Michael Black and Justices Bryan Beaumont and Robert French, and on 17 September they announced their reversal of North's decision, with Black opposing. Having won its appeal, the government was free to enact its "Pacific solution," and the *Manoora* was free to continue its voyage to variously distribute the rescuees to yet-to-be-built camps in Nauru and Papua New Guinea.

For Chief Justice Black and Justice French, the central question was the existence or otherwise of a sovereign power, an ancient prerogative, to repel friendly aliens. Such a prerogative, if it existed for the Australian sovereign, had never been exercised. Chief Justice Black refers to a footnote in William Holdsworth's *A History of English Law*:

> The last occasion on which it appears that a prerogative power to expel or exclude non-citizens [was used] was in 1771, when the Crown directed that Jews "unable to pay the usual freight," should, unless they had a passport from an ambassador, be excluded from the British territory.[5]

This prerogative, then, has its history, both of use and of disuse. And with this history of disuse comes one of the two important questions about the prerogative, that is, whether a prerogative not taken up by the executive continues to exist *potentially*. And if so, for how long? The unanswerability of the latter – for how long must a prerogative *not* be used before it ceases to have the potential *to* be used – meant that it was not specifically addressed in the judgments. Yet Black argued that, because it had not been used, the right to assert such a prerogative was questionable in law.

The second important question about this ancient prerogative, from a legal standpoint, was its relation to statute. That is to say, if such a prerogative exists, can it be exercised arbitrarily by any executing power, or must it be cast into a legislative form that directs how and by whom it may be deployed? Furthermore, where statutes exist that *do* cover the area of such a power, do they then *limit* the power of the sovereign or the executive to act on that prerogative *beyond the boundaries* of what is granted statutorily, that is, in legislation?

In the case under consideration, where the prerogative is the right to expel strangers at the border, the relevant statute is the *Migration Act 1958 (Cth)*. The *Act* seems to cover the grounds of the power in question, and hence to render moot the question whether the ancient prerogative remains in force. But since the *Act* does not make legal the kind of detention inflicted upon those on board the *Tampa*, the government needed to continue to assert that it *could* act by prerogative. And it further needed to argue that the *Act* did not curtail any powers granted to the executive by this prerogative. It was on this question that Chief Justice Black and Justice French disagreed.

For Chief Justice Black, the existence of the *Migration Act 1958 (Cth)*, and the extensive powers added to it by the *Border Protection Legislation Amendment Act 1999 (Cth)*, made clear that, whatever arguments there might be for an ancient prerogative, parliament had intended through this legislation to thoroughly codify such powers. Given that the 1999 Amendment granted the power to chase and to fire at or into a foreign ship, the extensive scope of the *Act* could not be clearer. If, given these extensive powers, the actions of the government in relation to the *Tampa* could still not be authorized with reference to the *Migration Act 1958 (Cth)*, then no prerogative *in addition to* what was granted statutorily by that *Act* could be relied upon to justify this detention. Black cited Lord Dunedin:

> [I]t is equally certain that if the whole ground of something which could be done by the prerogative is covered by the statute, it is the statute that rules. On this point I think the observation of the learned Master of the Rolls is unanswerable. He says: "What use would there be in imposing limitations, if the Crown could at its pleasure disregard them and fall back on prerogative?"[6]

The prerogative is not a whole of which the statute merely consumes a part. Rather, the fact that legislation has been made eliminates the right to appeal to any prior, or higher, prerogative power.

Justice French drew the opposite conclusion. He argued first of all for the existence of the prerogative, providing several citations to the effect that it is a fundamental right of a state or nation to expel aliens. He also asserted that this right may be grounded not simply in ancient tradition but in the essence of democratic sovereignty:

> Australia's status as a sovereign nation is reflected in its power to determine who may come into its territory and who may not and who shall be admitted into the Australian community and who shall not. That power may also be linked to the foundation of the Constitution in popular sovereignty implied in the agreement of the "people" of the pre-federation colonies "to unite in one indissoluble federal Commonwealth." It may be said that the people, through the structures of representative democracy for which the Constitution provides, including an executive responsible to the parliament, may determine who will or will not enter Australia.[7]

The fact that these words echo the Prime Minister's constant refrain during this period – "We will decide who comes to this country and the circumstances in which they come" – does not invalidate them. Indeed, on what grounds could they be invalidated, at least within an acceptance of popular sovereignty and the legal propriety of the foundation of the Constitution? Only, perhaps, on the grounds of an ancient obligation to accept strangers in distress. And to assert this obligation too strongly, not at sea but on land and within a "sovereign nation," threatens to tell a democracy what it can and cannot do to protect its borders, that is, itself.

Neither did Justice French agree that the *Migration Act 1958 (Cth)* abrogated this sovereign prerogative. The *Act*, he said, is facultative: it *confers* power. "It does not in the specific area evidence an intention to take it away."[8] In other words, if a prerogative power exists, and if no legislation removes that power, then it continues to exist. He therefore concluded that those steps taken by the government in preventing the *Tampa* from entering the migration zone "were within the scope of executive power."

The *Migration Act 1958 (Cth)* may not grant such a right, but nothing removes it, and specifically not the argument that it constituted unlawful detention. The government had argued that the

detention was not unlawful because the ship could travel anywhere in the world – *except here*. That the ship's captain refused
to travel anywhere other than Australia so long as the detainees
remained on board did not make the government responsible for
their confinement within the borders of the vessel.

Chief Justice Black argued against this logic with the following
analogy:

> To take a practical example on different facts, the circumstance that
> a person has decided to shut the door of a room, and to keep it
> shut, can surely provide no answer to a claim against another person
> who, knowing of those facts, then closes the only other door with
> its consequence that the people inside cannot get out.[9]

That is, although the government knew that Arne Rinnan had shut
the door out of Australia, it nevertheless decided to keep closed the
only other door out of the *Tampa*. Justice French, however, did not
accept that the government had thereby detained.

> Their inability to go elsewhere derived from circumstances which
> did not come from any action on the part of the Commonwealth.[10]

The arrangements that the government made, including the presence of SAS troops on board the *Tampa*, were done for humanitarian purposes (according, then, to an ancient obligation), and any
detaining effect was merely incidental.

> Those arrangements did not constitute a restraint upon freedom
> attributable to the Commonwealth given the fact that the captain of
> the MV Tampa would not sail out of Australia while the rescuees were
> on board. In my opinion, taken as a whole, there was no restraint
> on their liberty which could be attributed to the Commonwealth.[11]

Such is the way of law.

The third judge, Justice Beaumont, was not overly concerned
with questions about the ancient prerogative to repel aliens. What
made Beaumont's judgment interesting was its relation to the
material facts, to the material situation that was being played out

during the hearing of the case before Justice North. The version of the ancient prerogative with which Beaumont was concerned was phrased the other way around: *there can be no absolute right of strangers, enemy or friendly, to enter our borders.* Whether the sovereign may prevent this entry in any particular way, the aliens themselves have no particular right to demand that they be allowed in.

Justice Beaumont was concerned with this way of framing the issue because what taxed his judicial mind was not whether the government had the right to prevent the *Tampa* from landing. Rather, he was concerned with whether *Justice North* had the jurisdiction to demand that the rescuees, now aboard the *Manoora* and outside Australian territory, be brought *back* into that territory and onto the Australian mainland. His conclusion was simply that, having no enforceable legal right to *enter* Australia, and having *left*, no court could order their return, whether that was their intended original destination or not:

> That is to say, whatever questions may arise as to the power to deport without legislative backing [. . .] there is nothing in any of the authorities to contradict the principle that an alien has no common law right to *enter* Australia. This aspect is beyond argument. For this reason alone, I would allow the appeal.[12]

Thus, as soon as the deal was struck to allow the transfer to the *Manoora*, and as soon as that Australian government vessel had left Australian waters, no power existed that could allow a judge to compel the *return* of the rescuees (ignoring the fact, however, that when the transfer to the *Manoora* was agreed to, it was on condition that the rescuees *would* be returned should the case be lost). It is unclear whether the argument used by Justice Beaumont had occurred to the government at the time it negotiated this transfer on humanitarian grounds to a military troopship. But undoubtedly its instincts were that the further from Australia these 433 people could be placed, the less likely it was that anything could force them back.

The truth, of course, is that these people were detained, deliberately and remarkably. Their detention continued when they disembarked from the *Manoora*, in a manner that continued to be organized and controlled by the Australian government, and at great cost. Of course, detention without reason is as unlawful in the sovereign states of Nauru and Papua New Guinea as it is in Australia. For that reason, in order to avoid writs of *habeas corpus* in those countries, special legal schemes needed to be invented. In Nauru, for example, as David Marr and Marian Wilkinson explain, they were not detainees at all.

> They would be visitors to Nauru on special visas which were issued on condition that each person remained within the confines of a camp.[13]

Rather than detainees, rather than illegal immigrants, rather than asylum seekers, when the rescuees arrived on Nauru, their status was as tourists, on a tour, *exclusively*, of a camp set up and paid for by the Australian government.

The court case and its appeal were essentially unconcerned with the marine obligation to rescue those in distress. There was no reason to be so concerned because it was not in dispute. Yet what most clearly reveals that the Australian government did indeed detain those rescued by the *Tampa* is the failure of the government to adhere to the dictates of such an obligation. The obligation does not end with Arne Rinnan plucking people from the sea. The entire purpose of removing people from the sea is so that their lives may continue, so that a future is possible. If they are not to live forever on board the vessel which rescues them, then eventually they must set foot on land. If captains are obligated to rescue all souls, regardless of origin, even at the risk of overcrowding their own vessel, then surely this is with the understanding that those rescued will be permitted to disembark.

It was stated earlier that marine transportation has been transformed into a planetary system. It is a vast economic and technical apparatus that both works with national and territorial borders, and adjusts itself to the demands of the borderless ocean. Once again, borders are very different things depending upon whether one is speaking about capital or citizenry (or, indeed, in even more directly Marxist terms, capital or labor). But, even today, the enormous vessels of this system require captains and seafarers, and these global laborers are of course routinely afforded the right to disembark at port. To deny this right to even temporary disembarkation, to deny rescuees the right to land, is to deny the very obligation to rescue. As such, however ingenious the Pacific Solution may have seemed to those cunning enough to devise and execute it, and even if no souls were lost, the actions of the government in relation to those in distress at sea was to deny the right to life.

Chapter 6

Enemy Combatants

Historians debate whether the first camps to appear were the *campos de concentrationes* created by the Spanish in Cuba in 1896 to suppress the popular insurrection of the colony, or the "concentration camps" into which the English herded the Boers toward the start of the century. What matters here is that in both cases, a state of emergency linked to a colonial war is extended to an entire civil population. The camps are thus born not out of ordinary law (even less, as one might have supposed, from a transformation and development of criminal law) but out of a state of exception and martial law. *Giorgio Agamben*[1]

At the end of the nineteenth century the United States of America was preoccupied with war. The Spanish–American War of 1898 was no great military affair, unwished for by the governments of either nation, and featured little in the way of important battles. Yet the war was a significant early demonstration of the power the United States had achieved, and as an indication of the future directions that power would take. It made clear that no European power would be able to defend any territory in the Americas against United States military aggression. Having made its demonstration clear, America did not hold back from dominating the region.

The war was largely a battle for Cuba, fought between the old empire that controlled things politically (Spain), and the emerging empire that already controlled Cuba economically (America). Just as the European aristocracy had to succumb to the economic power of the emergent European bourgeoisie, so too the Spanish empire was forced to yield to the superior might of American industry. The apparent and superficial reasons for war seem to be merely pretexts for a reckoning that with hindsight appears to have been inevitable. The sinking of the battleship *Maine* on 15 February 1898, for instance, with the loss of 260 officers and men, was the major precipitating event. It is now considered likely not to have been an act of aggression at all, but rather the result of an accidental explosion. And the contribution of the Hearst and Pulitzer press sensationalism to an atmosphere favorable to igniting conflict seems retrospectively to have been the *means* by which war was achieved. But the war itself, insofar as it was the expulsion of an imperial power from Cuba in favor of an economic power, appears in hindsight to have been inevitable.

This is of course a false sense of history. Wars are never bound to happen. Yet the sequence in which the accidents of history occur frequently seems more than merely random. If the assassination of the Archduke Ferdinand was an accidental catalyst for European conflagration in 1914, it was also the culmination of the building of a mood, a "metaphysic," that war was imminent and inevitable, as Robert Musil has so amply testified.

Prior to the sinking of the *Maine* America had about it something of that sense of the building of a metaphysic, of a hunger for war. The competition for headlines between the two major newspaper conglomerates led to ever more lurid accounts of Spanish corruption and cruelty in Cuba. In spite of Spain's eventual willingness to accede to virtually all the American demands, success without war was not a tempting enough prospect for either the American people or President McKinley. In the end he acquiesced to the wishes of the populace for an outbreak of hostilities. Presidents have learned to make their demands of other nations impossible enough such that the decision to go to war may be reserved in presidential rather than foreign hands. McKinley, like subsequent Presidents, if given a choice, preferred to be dictated to by domestic journalists rather than alien tyrants.

Whatever sensationalism was involved in the Hearst and Pulitzer coverage of Cuba, the Spaniards displayed ruthlessness in controlling Cuban insurgents. General Valeriano Weyler y Nicolau, in particular, added substance to the sensationalism, with his policy of "*reconcentrado.*" In order to control the insurgents in the Cuban countryside, General Weyler invented the strategy of forcibly moving the entire rural population into suburban camps where they could be controlled. These camps caused great suffering and the deaths of tens of thousands of Cubans, both from famine and from the fact that the camps were conducive to the spread of disease.

What makes them *concentration camps* in the sense we understand today, however, is not merely the fact of suffering, but the *intention* behind them. The Spanish military authorities conceived an entire population as open to technical means of concentration and control, and a technical apparatus for these purposes was then invented. Like the concentration camps of National Socialist Germany, the policy of *reconcentrado* was not really a military strategy at all, but the reduction of human populations to stock, to be herded and shipped, corralled and incarcerated. It was a policy, after all, conceived and implemented not during a war, but rather in the *aftermath* of the Ten Years War in Cuba. It was a way of organizing a population for the sake of the security and sovereignty of the imperial power.

President McKinley's ultimatum to Spain included the demand that the concentration camp policy be rescinded. Spain accepted the measure, but the drive to war was already unstoppable. It is timely to note, however, that one of the forces driving America into war in 1898 was the abhorrence of the American people at the thought of Spanish concentration camps in Cuba. Whatever other reasons there were for war, and however the media of the day misrepresented the situation in Cuba, that cauldron of reasons included outrage at an imperial power concentrating and controlling a subjugated population. Whatever invisible economic hand was forcing the government into war, it was *also* democracy acting against tyranny, and in particular against the tyranny that treats populations according to the methods of modern industry.

The consequence of the Spanish–American War was Cuban independence, but this was achieved only with great American reluctance, and at a cost. Having acted for the Cubans against the Spanish, the United States would have liked to annex the territory, but in the end permitted independence. Nevertheless there was one part of Cuban territory that America succeeded in holding onto, formalized by treaty in 1903. That piece of territory would allow America always to retain the potential for military action in Cuba, and to maintain naval control of the surrounding area. That piece of territory was Guantanamo Bay, a fine deepwater port in the south of Cuba.

Guantanamo

What is the status of Guantanamo Bay? The treaty that granted control and "sovereignty" to America over the Cuban port was a political instrument, but it was also economic. The United States agreed to lease the port from Cuba for $2000 per year, and this was later increased to its current level, $4035 per year. Such a figure is, of course, a repetition of the old practice of purchasing nations from the natives for a few beads and blankets, then using this as the economico-juridical foundation for a "properly constituted" sovereignty. The Guantanamo lease is unusual for two reasons, firstly because it was granted in perpetuity, as opposed, say, to the arrangements for Hong Kong, Macao and the Panama Canal. It is now more than 100 years old. The second reason is that the landlord, the Cuban government, has never cashed a rent cheque. Cuba has consistently and continually objected to the arrangement, to which it initially agreed (and to which it recommitted itself in 1934), on the grounds that the agreement was reached when Cuba was in a helpless and desperate state. Cuba further argues that modern international law surrounding treaties would not validate the enforceability of such an arrangement. It is thus a lease "agreement" that lasts forever, for which no money changes hands, and to which the lessor objects.

Guantanamo Bay was thus the pound of flesh that America demanded of Cuba for the gift of independence. That democracy acts against tyranny is admirable, but precisely because it is *democracy* acting, the consideration of the "national interest" demands recompense for this virtue. If the recipients of that virtue are not grateful for the gift bestowed upon them, they must suffer the cost that accompanies the gift. Especially if the democracy that acts virtuously is of an order of magnitude more powerful than the one for whom she acts. For over a century, then, the port has been American territory and the site of an American naval base, as stipulated by the terms of the treaty.

The more remarkable irony, however, is that today the United States finds it necessary to insist that Guantanamo Bay is not under American sovereignty at all, is not American territory, and that the American presence there is to be understood as equivalent to a guest taking a room at a Havana tourist hotel. The naval base was used to detain both Haitians and Cubans for the purposes of immigration control. In this way, the base functioned in a manner equivalent to those territorial regions such as Christmas Island that the Australian government "excised" from its "migration zone." Such procedures are a way of placing a territory into a kind of legal haze, at least as far as immigration law is concerned. By holding potential immigrants in such a zone of legal indeterminacy, decisions about the future direction of their journey can be made at greater leisure and without the same risks of legal objection. If asylum seekers can be caught in such a net, then they can be effectively filtered away, since they have neither made it to territorial shores, nor sought entry to that territory through "legitimate" migration programs.

After 11 September 2001 and the ensuing war in Afghanistan, however, the United States has made use of Guantanamo Bay in a fashion that extends far beyond what was understood to be the case for the Haitians and Cubans held there pending immigration determination. The American prize for its outrage at Spanish concentration camps in Cuba has become the right to run its own camp on the same territory. The fact that the United States has the power to do what it does, that it can move people from one country into another because *it decides to* and because it *cannot be prevented from doing so*, should not prevent consideration of the significance of such acts.

Afghanistan

The war against the Taliban in Afghanistan was of course provoked by the al Qaeda attacks of 11 September 2001. The reasons for this war are not difficult to understand. Perhaps the most obvious and most immediate political implication of that day was that a war would follow. There was no possibility of avoiding war. Missile attacks such as those Clinton launched against Iraq, and even air campaigns along the lines of that unleashed against

Yugoslavia, would never suffice. After 11 September it was clear that a "real" war, with a "real" victory, was required. Required by whom? First of all by the American people. No president faced with the singular situation orchestrated by al Qaeda in 2001 could resist the will of the people for retaliation. Any President that did resist such a "need" of the people, any President that failed to rise to the theatre and drama of the situation, would doubtless face an onslaught from political opponents requiring resignation from office. With President George W Bush there was never any risk that such a strategy of avoiding war would be attempted.

Bush cannot really be blamed for this. If there was never any doubt that war would follow the attacks, then this is primarily because *democracy* demanded it. The will of the people, combined with the machinations of political process, responded catalytically to the terrorist provocation. The inevitability of this outcome is unfortunate, even from the perspective of those whose singular goal is to defeat the al Qaeda strategy. In all the thousands of pages written about bin Laden in the popular media, it is surprising how little attention is given to the *reason* for the 11 September attacks. It is not sufficient to point toward hatred of America, nor even to the long history of international injustices perpetrated or facilitated by the United States. Given the level of planning and calculation involved, it is inconceivable that these attacks were not also a piece in an overall strategy. And the inevitability and predictability of a retaliatory war implies that it was most likely part of the calculations of the 11 September terrorists themselves.

That is, the intention was to *provoke* retaliation and war. The question then becomes why al Qaeda would wish to see American attacks in the Middle East. The most likely answer is to galvanise Muslims toward a radicalism or extremism that would make possible the establishment of Islamic states in the Middle East and elsewhere. There is nothing new about such a suggestion, but it goes for the most part unstated in the Western coverage of 11 September and its aftermath.

For the American government, the impossibility of avoiding *war* meant the *necessity* of avoiding any public examination of the terrorists' intentions. The one sure thing about the attacks was that the perpetrators intended to provoke a response (and the bigger the better). But the dissemination of this thought or reflection upon it threatened the legitimacy of a war in the minds of an American public already hungry for it. Al Qaeda could only be understood *publicly* in terms of evil, not in terms of strategy. They could only be understood in terms of hatred and as the enemy, the enemy of freedom, of democracy, of America. The strategic thought behind the attacks was not of interest to an Administration concerned, in the days after the attack, not with *what* to do, but with *whom* to do it to.

As proponents of the war against Afghanistan love to say to its opponents, how is it possible to object to the removal of the Taliban? How can one miss a government devoted, in an extraordinary way and by all reports, to horrifying barbarism? And there is very little answer to such questions. The war against the Taliban was comparatively cheap and effective and, despite the uncertainties about the future of Afghanistan, it still seems clear that the worst outcome (which remains possible) would be the return of the Taliban. But one cannot object to the removal of a regime on the grounds that it might come back.

The only problem with this line of reasoning is that the war was not prosecuted in order to topple the Taliban. It is indeed the case that once war in Afghanistan was decided upon, nothing less than the annihilation of the Taliban government (which is different from the annihilation of the Taliban themselves) would have been acceptable to the US Administration. Nevertheless this was really only a welcome by-product of the real intention, which was, simply, to satisfy the desire for action. This makes a difference. The war was not, any more than Gulf War II, any more than the Spanish–American War, conducted out of a sense of virtue, but out of a need for war itself. The proof of this is simple: when the object of that war, Osama bin Laden, failed to appear at the correct moment in the narrative, it became necessary to turn attention to potential wars elsewhere (which is not to say that war in Iraq had not been pre-planned). And with this distraction of attention from Afghanistan came an almost complete American indifference to the fate of the Afghan people in the aftermath of their liberation.

The need for war

To speak of a need for war is not quite the same thing as reducing the fact of war to a psychological necessity. It is not a matter of a collective human nature, a group psyche devoted to violence and destruction. It is not that all conflict is essentially the same, and thus that the creaking into action of the lumbering and massive American war machine is *simply* one more repetition in the endless human history of tribal warfare. It may be possible to make a case that war has been and always will be a fact of human existence, as long as this existence is organized into different groups. But already this is not quite the same thing as the mere invocation of human nature.

What differentiates war from the fighting that individuals engage in amongst each other? Why is war a name we give only to a human activity, despite the fact that groups of animals frequently engage in conflict within the same species? War is never a matter of individuals but of groups. War is the outcome of difference *and* identity. It depends, therefore, on a border. The border might not be a fence or a wall, but it must nevertheless in some way be *marked*. The border of difference and identity, the line in the sand dividing us and them, must be able to be *recognized*. That war is possible, according to such an idea, depends upon the operation of some kind of technical *separation*. Before the group, there must be the *border* upon which is grounded the separation *into* groups of same and different.

War is thus a political phenomenon, in that it depends upon the existence of separated groups. It requires groups that experience themselves *as* groups, that is, whose individuals experience each other as *connected*, and as disconnected from non-members. But if war is thus political, it has its origin in the *pre*-political fact of the possibility of establishing borders. It is this possibility, in the *technics* of this possibility, that politics finds *its* possibility.

Of course animals mark their territory, and may also divide themselves into groups. Human war, however, as opposed to the conflicts that occur between animals, is distinguished by the use of weaponry and organization. War means the possibility of inventing and deploying weaponry, and the possibility of deploying human beings in an organized way *as* weapons. This is the lesson of the so-called "*hoplite* reform" of ancient Greece. This was the transformation of the method of fighting from one based around the heroic perfor-mance of individuals, as exemplified in *The Iliad*, to an organized arrangement of infantry in battle. The discovery that having soldiers act as one mass meant a decisive military advantage was not only the foundation of modern war as the technical arrangement of peo-ple and weaponry for the purposes of combat. It was also the birth of a fundamental Greek metaphor for the political. If humanity is the political animal, this is first of all because of this possibility for technical organization, and the capacity for invention, technics, and organization in general.

Still, what does it mean to speak of a "need" for war? War has the grounds of its possibility in the borders between groups. For a group to undertake warfare it must be able to recognize itself as *within* the boundaries that make it a group. Once the boundary exists, once it is marked, the group may recognize itself, and *therefore* may rec-ognize itself as *threatened*. Once a group exists, it becomes possible for those members *of* the group to see themselves as engaged in a struggle for survival against outsiders. Fundamentally, the reason for war, insofar as it is a matter of reason, is always the struggle for survival, however removed from such struggles any particular war may seem.

That there is a border means there is a group. That there is a group means that group may see itself as threatened. That a group there-fore sees itself in a struggle for survival means it must grant to itself the possibility of making *decisions*, that is, first of all, the decision to go to war. This is the essential tie between borders, war, and sovereignty. Democracy was conceived, traditionally, as the aboli-tion of the politics of absolute sovereignty. Whatever truth there is to such a notion, however, it is also the mask democracy has given to itself without ever shedding the need for absolute sovereignty. That is, there is no sovereignty that does not keep the potential for being absolute. There is no *decision* if there is not absolute decision. Thus sovereignty may be given up or watered down in the face of international agreements or economic integration. But lying behind such withering of sovereignty is, for every bordered group that sees itself as such, the right, granted to itself, to make a decision, to act sovereignly *when it is absolutely necessary*.

That is, national sovereignty is like individual sovereignty according to Hobbes. The individual may grant the existence of law, may agree to give up all kinds of decisions to the law of the sovereign, but it is impossible for law to take away the sovereign right of the individual to *resist death*. Even where individuals grant to the law the right to decide on life and death, nothing can ever take away the right of the individual to fight against their own homicide. And this is true because there is no power which *could* take it away, nothing that the law could hold over an individual already faced with his or her own death. All accession to law finds its limit in *this* sovereign right of the individual.[2]

For Hobbes, to speak of "rights" means only to speak of this most basic situation of the mortal individual. Only in the work of later political philosophers are rights extended and dispersed, and, in the process, removed from any grounding in the facts of mortal life. It is only in Hobbes that rights are not simply a matter of law in its *transcendence* from nature, but rather more like a logical consequence of the nature of the individual's existence as such. It is only in the extreme situation, in the fight against death, that the "right" of the individual to conduct this fight, to resist death, emerges, and as it does all other "law" dissolves to triviality. Likewise, any group, any nation, whatever treaties and conventions it *decides* to be bound by, always reserves the right to defend itself against the possibility of oblivion and annihilation.

For this reason war has always been something of a problem for modern democracies, and perhaps also for ancient ones. Democracy, of course, is nothing other than a means of making decisions, of determining the decisions of a group. In this sense, democracy has always meant a reconfiguring of the traditional notion of sovereignty rather than its abolition. But the *way* of deciding makes a difference, and makes a difference first of all when it is what matters most, when it is a matter of survival.

The methodological problem democracy finds in war is that, in order to be conducted *effectively*, war needs to be a matter of executive decision. It demands an executive *free* to make decisions purely on the grounds of strategic effectiveness. It demands a sovereign. War cannot be effectively prosecuted by the legislature. This is not only because of the speed of executive decisions compared with legislative decision-making. It is also because war *always* depends, to some extent, on secrecy and surprise, and thus cannot cope with the transparency that democracy apparently demands. The right to keep secrets that democratic governments grant to themselves in the name of "national interest" is, however frequently it is abused for political purposes, always based in the logic of warfare.

Democracies have always been keen to resolve the contradiction between the sovereignty of the people and the sovereign logic of warfare. The very split between executive and legislature is a figure of this attempt at resolution. The fact that often the "command" of the armed forces is granted constitutionally to the head of state is a recognition of the need for a sovereignty capable of living up to the demands of survival. In the extreme situation, when it is a question of a threat profound enough to demand war, the sovereign must be free to act. This freedom to act means the freedom to act technocratically, according to what expert military strategists believe to be those tactics most likely to succeed. In wartime the sovereign *must* listen, not to the people first, but to his or her generals and advisors. Such is *democratic* theory. It is the seriousness of war, the seriousness of the consequences of failure, that demand this.

But, precisely because of this seriousness, democracy is confronted with the dangers of *removing* wartime decisions from the hands of the people. Recognition of this can be found, for example, in the requirement of the American Constitution that *Congress* must vote to go to war. When the life and death of the group is at stake, how could war *ever* be taken from the hands of the people, whose lives and deaths are the ones at stake?

And, obviously enough, it is not only the decision to *go* to war that should involve the people. The strategic decisions made at every moment during a wartime situation carry the same significance as does the war itself, for the consequences of error may be just as catastrophic. The risk in granting the sovereign special rights in wartime is that the democratic institutions become nothing but the means of deciding all those details of life *except* questions of survival. Parliament is then just a forum for deciding on the *form* that life within the group takes, without the capacity for deciding on the fundamental questions *of* democratic life itself.

The difficulty of resolving this question of the relation between democracy and war can be seen in the relation of warfare to elections in modern parliamentary democracy. During lengthy wars (World War II, for instance) elections may be held right in the middle of important battles. There is something fundamentally odd about conducting an electoral campaign and a military campaign simultaneously. War must then either become a "political issue" or the opposing parties must agree to avoid this. In the first case, there emerges the possibility, which is after all properly democratic, that military strategy is decided by vote. In the second case, the democratic participants have agreed to sacrifice the democratic right to disagreement on the grounds of military necessity. In either case, the disjunction between popular and military sovereignty is something a democracy "manages" at times of crisis, rather than resolves.

It is a problem that becomes more acute with technological development and as the speed of war increases. Since World War II American presidents have been reluctant to allow Congress to declare war, and hence the wars since then have not "legally" been wars in American terms. More than that, the decision to go to war, of *when* to go to war, and of *how* to conduct war, has been profoundly influenced by matters of timing. Wars have been commenced almost always with a view toward avoiding any overlap with presidential election campaigns, because of the political *and* the military difficulties such an overlap would cause. With such avoidance it becomes possible to maintain the illusion that military decisions are an executive rather than a fully democratic problem.

In short, democracy is torn by war. War is on the one hand at the heart of democracy. War is the possible necessity that emerges from the very constitution of the group, the very decision to institute the borders that found the group. As soon as there is a group, the question of the survival of the group arises, and the possible necessity of war is *the* first political question. On the other hand war means the requirement that the sovereign act *sovereignly*, that is, freely. War demands decisions that are made with speed, according to the rationality of military strategy and military logic. Behind all technocracy lies the logic of warfare.

The possibility of war, the possibility of a struggle for survival, makes democracy insecure, unsure of itself. The fact that democracy *succeeds* more or less in managing the problem of warfare should not blind us to the existence of the *difficulty* for democracy that war causes.

The *possibility* of future war makes democracy insecure about its *type* of sovereignty. Faced with the most extreme emergency, has democracy the will or the way to respond appropriately and effectively? Can annihilation be staved off with elections, with Senate committees and transparent government, or does it not demand the force of genuine *leadership*? The possibility of being thrown into a situation in which the survival of the group is at stake leads to the feeling that to institute democracy too closely resembles the *renunciation* of the right to sovereign decision in the extreme situation. The thought of democracy as a sort of renunciation gives it a bloodless, lifeless, mechanical appearance that, for example, fuelled the hatred of Weimar democracy by its domestic opponents. In that context, taking on the burden of war is a matter of reasserting one's sovereignty, reasserting the ability of the group to determine its existence. War becomes the proof of the group's capacity for existence, and therefore of its *right* to exist. War is a narcissistic act, a proof granted to oneself of one's worth, a proof that one *is*.

And this is the point. If the group begins with the border, with the marking of the border, then it begins with an act. The group begins with the act that establishes the group, and yet the group must already have supposed itself *to* exist in order to decide upon the institution *of* the border. There is an uncertainty in all institution of borders, in all constitution of groups. The institution of the border is an *excessive* act, an act that determines the certainty of the group over and above what was in fact determinable. The institution of the border, the constitution of the group, is excessive because what is established is only true *retrospectively*. The moment that sovereignty is established requires a *sovereign* decision – the decision to institute the border – a sovereign decision that should only be possible *after* what is instituted becomes fact. Sovereignty is always a kind of impossibility, the aftermath of an act in excess of what is possible. It is always bought on credit.

And thus sovereignty is always in need of reaffirmation. There is something uncertain, insecure, about sovereignty. War is not only a matter of survival in the sense of a simply conservative closed loop, a circle of hunger and satisfaction. War, like the institution of sovereignty itself, is excessive. It is the interest paid against the initial loan with which sovereignty was first purchased. War is the confirmation of the sovereignty of the group, the confirmation that the group continues to hold in its hands the possibility of decisive and successful *action* when it comes to survival. It is the confirmation that its sovereignty is actual. The need for war is not only the need to reassure an uneasy population that it has not paralyzed its will by agreeing to act only democratically, that is, only according to the weak decision-making of the legislature. The decision to go to war is also the *repetition* of the decision to institute the border, the narcissistic and excessive act that indeed confirms that there is sovereignty.

If the United States has been a nation that has needed war, this has been because it has needed to assert the fact of its sovereignty. This is not, obviously, because it is a weak nation trying to convince itself of its strength. Nor is it because it is a nation uncertain of the legitimacy of its foundation. Rather, the very *strength* and *security* of American sovereignty on this planet seems to create the need constantly to put this sovereignty to the test, as though it is almost unbelievable, as though another power *must* be hiding, haunting America, waiting to emerge and unveil the illusion of that sovereignty.

After 11 September 2001 America needed war. After a dramatic blow to its narcissism, after a blow to the sense that its borders offered protection, America needed to reassure itself of its sovereignty. That is, it needed to reconfirm its capacity for decision, for decisive action, to prove its ability to respond to the extreme situation, the situation where existence is at stake. If 11 September was not in fact the day on which the United States was confronted with such a situation, it was at least the day on which America *imagined* or fantasized about that situation. On that day America was projected or projected itself into a possible future where its time ran out, where its future ended. The United States is both more and less certain about its sovereignty than any other nation, which is why it is more willing and finds it more necessary to go to war. On 11 September 2001 America felt its sovereignty was put to the test, and thus felt challenged to respond with a sovereign act. Only war would meet this challenge.

The war against the Taliban was thus the narcissistic war that re-established the certainty of American existence. Even if this certainty risked being undermined by the puniness of the opponent and the swiftness of victory, nevertheless it was a war undertaken to assert the border that marks American identity in opposition to its other. It was thus a war of sovereignty, conducted in the name of and for the cause of American sovereignty. It joined, therefore, that great tradition of wars conducted since the rise of modern democracy. It is tempting to say that it was a war like any other, smaller perhaps, but essentially just another symptom of the perpetual return of American bellicosity, of the American need for the assertion of its sovereignty. Yet it was also a war that marked a certain process of the transformation of sovereignty. Perhaps this transformation was already underway, or had even been underway for some time, but even so it was in the aftermath of the war against Afghanistan that it first became acutely visible.

After the fall

War is that violent process conducted by states in which human law is so utterly suspended that the massive extermination of human life is decided upon as though it were merely a technical and strategic problem. Thus in war anything is possible. Nevertheless war has never, or hardly ever, been *only* a matter of the annihilation of the other. In ancient Greece, when an invasion was successful all the men of the conquered city would be slaughtered, but etiquette meant that the women and children were merely enslaved. In our more civilized times etiquette demands that prisoners of war not be killed at all, and that they are returned home at the conclusion of hostilities. And those treaties and conventions that proclaim what are oxymoronically called the "laws of war" specifically define the prisoner of war as requiring a military uniform or some distinguishing costume that identifies them as belonging to an opposing belligerent group. In this way these "laws" are intended to exclude from imprisonment all those "civilians" that are habitually caught up in the heat of battle.

It is these "laws" among others that the United States decided could not be followed during the war against Afghanistan, nor in the aftermath of the fall of the Taliban. Having succeeded grandly in the aim of removing the Taliban from government, America decided that it could not return several hundreds of those it had captured, whether they wore identifying uniforms or whether they did not. Mirroring the Spanish response to the Ten Years War, it was *after* the conclusion of hostilities in the Afghan theatre of war that America decided to construct its concentration camps in Cuba. The vast majority of those prisoners transferred to camps at Guantanamo were not members of any warring army and wore no identifying markings. This absence ought to guarantee return, according to the Geneva convention, at the completion of hostilities. But this absence, which is not only an absence of uniforms but an absence of *membership* in an enemy army, was the very ground used by America to justify their continuing internment. Because these prisoners are not members of an opposing army, the American government argues, they cannot be treated according to the rules of the Geneva convention, nor according to any other rules or laws. They belong to an entirely other category, the so-called "enemy combatants."

Such "logic" is of course tortured and in fact absurd. But the logic behind the "logic" is clear. It is this: although the war against the Taliban gave the appearance of being a war like any other, in fact it was not. It was not a war against the people of Afghanistan, nor even against the "state" of Afghanistan, because the Taliban "regime" was not granted the legitimacy of a state. The war *looked like* an ordinary war because it is difficult for war to take on new forms. It looked like an ordinary war because we have yet to invent or discover how the new wars will look, because we have not yet learned to recognize their appearance. Or even, most radically, it had the appearance of an ordinary war because that is what the people (of the United States) needed. They needed to see a *war*, an enemy state vanquished, a victory flag raised.

The War on Terror

But it was not an ordinary war, because it was merely the first battle in the War on Terror. The first significance of *this* war is that it is not merely against other states. It is a war against an enemy, often invisible, that flourishes in many states, that may be found anywhere and everywhere, that operates in secrecy, in cells and through networks. There is a precedent for such a war. It is that component of the National Socialist strategy that constituted the war against the Jews. Like that war, the War on Terror is a perpetual struggle, or a struggle that does not cease until the enemy is utterly defeated and annihilated. And this is a terminus that can be determined *only* by "us," for no capitulation of the enemy could ever satisfy the need for complete and utter victory.

Of course there are differences. Unlike the Nazis during the Second World War, America does not intend to simply exterminate a racial group it has deemed to be nothing but a parasite and vermin. There is no racial or biological rhetoric about the threat to the purity of the master race. There will be no mass gas chambers, and there will not be millions of deaths. And, of course, the Jews were an enemy of the Germans in fantasy only, whereas al Qaeda has been very successful in carrying out real and deadly attacks in America and on American targets. These differences are not small. Indeed, they are massive, and to ignore them would be to contribute to the forgetting of the terrible history of the extermination. If the racial logic and the exterminatory logic does not apply, however, what remains in common between the War on Terror and the war against the Jews is the logic of the "war": a potentially perpetual struggle against a dispersed enemy that cannot be reduced to any location in particular. Rather than a war against enemy states, what is involved is a war against the idea of an enemy, or an enemy idea, the idea of the dirty Jew or the idea of the evil terrorist.

The figure of the "enemy combatant," of the Camp X-ray or Camp Delta inmate, bears comparison, despite these differences, with the Auschwitz prisoner. This comparison, once again, cannot and must not be at the level of the *conditions* of imprisonment. Although the conditions at Guantanamo remain largely secret from the public, nevertheless there can be no doubt that they in no way resemble the conditions of the extermination camps run by the Nazis. For that matter, there is no doubt that the conditions are also infinitely superior to those of the camps in Spanish Cuba at the end of the nineteenth century. But what is fundamentally in common between these figures is that they are defined, by the sovereign, as falling under no legal jurisdiction other than the rule of the camp itself. The camp inmate, whether in Guantanamo or Auschwitz, has no legal existence beyond the law of the camp, a law that in both cases exists only by the decree of the sovereign. It is the significance of this fact that the situation in Guantanamo requires us to understand.

The camp

Adolf Hitler became chancellor of Germany on 30 January 1933. Dachau concentration camp opened on 20 March of the same year, three days before the enabling laws were enacted. Even in these early days of National Socialist government it was no Reichstag legislation that led to Dachau, but merely a decree of the chancellor, more than a year before Hitler granted himself the title "Führer." From the beginning the camps operated outside all other legal jurisdiction, and prisoners were without any legal recourse. As the Third Reich evolved, greater and greater legal significance was granted to decrees of the Führer, eventually to the point where this was the only effective legislative authority. And by the time of the Wannsee conference that decided upon the extermination of the Jews in 1942, no explicit decree but merely the understood will of the Führer was sufficient.

The president of the United States does not make law in the same way as the Führer. There is still Congress; there are still elections; there are still courts with the capacity for independent judgment. What is more, the question of legal jurisdiction in relation to Guantanamo inmates is still a matter to be arbitrated in the courts. But however this is finally decided, if it ever is, the position of the Administration has been from the beginning and continues to be that "enemy combatants" are without any legal recourse whatsoever, that they remain camp inmates by decree of the president, and that presidential whim is a sufficient legal foundation.

Any number of humanitarian and legal arguments may be raised against this state of affairs. That neither domestic law nor international treaty obligations apply to the "enemy combatants" effectively displaces them from even the most basic juridical sphere. The Administration has fought every step of the way, for instance, against the notion that *habeas corpus* could apply in this singular situation. The Guantanamo prisoners are, as far as the Administration is concerned, and like those condemned to the Nazi concentration camps, beyond the reach of any protective authority. And, therefore, there is nothing that it is impermissible to do *to* these inmates, whether it is torture or death, *except* by the grace of presidential decree. It must be noted that the last of these fates – execution – is one that the president and his Cabinet have insisted from the beginning to be within the realm of possible outcomes for the Guantanamo guests. We are assured that the former – torture – is not, although unlike execution the definition of torture is open to subjective interpretation.

It is difficult not to be disturbed by the position of the Administration in relation to Guantanamo. With no protection beyond that offered by presidential grace, these inmates appear to be reduced to possessing *nothing beyond* that Hobbesian concept of rights. They have the right to resist their own execution but nothing more, and that only because nothing could ever take it away. For those who live in a world where law operates as though it is eternally *there*, there is something utterly frightening about the prospect of being removed from all law. The notion that one could be lifted from the nation of which one is a citizen by the military of another, taken to a third country and imprisoned, without sentence, without trial, without charge, and without *law*, yet indefinitely, and with the very real possibility of execution at some indeterminate point in the future, all in the name of freedom, is a significant challenge to all existing legal and political thought. It is difficult to avoid the feeling that, without law, one is no longer a person at all.

It is thus with one voice that all those opposed to this situation cry out at the legal outrage of proclaiming a human being as being beyond the protection of any law. Lawyers and human rights activists agree that the horror of Guantanamo is the fact that the Administration takes it upon itself to ignore the patiently developed work of centuries of legal tradition and progress. And indeed there is something tragic about this willfulness on the part of the Administration. But there is something almost as troubling about an opposition to the Guantanamo camps on the grounds of law and humanitarianism. Would solid legal grounds make the camps acceptable? Would luxurious conditions, an absence of suicide attempts, and opportunities for education make them simply a question of "rehousing" in order to protect the American public?

That Guantanamo is a nicer place to be than Auschwitz has no guarantee other than one's faith that the President is a nicer guy than the Führer. Or that the American public cares enough about these people at least to oppose an extermination camp, if not an execution camp. Although secrecy shrouds Guantanamo, and we cannot presume to know what does or does not occur there, the more visceral forms of torture may have been avoided. The medical assistance available to the prisoners is, furthermore, probably of a higher standard than many of them could hope for at home. Perhaps a team of psychiatrists maintains their mental health as well as can be expected given the circumstances, if such a concept retains any meaning there. But this "improvement" in camp conditions since the time of Auschwitz seems not to stem from the idea of prisoners' rights, but rather from a development of the notion of the camp itself, an increase in its effectiveness. To permit the health of prisoners to deteriorate would simply be an unnecessary burden upon the smooth functioning of the camp itself. For, even if they are without rights, the logic of the camp demands the security and protection not only of those who are protected *from* the camp inmates, but the security and protection of those inmates themselves, even if one day this culminates in their equally efficient elimination.

The nature of law

Arguing against Guantanamo on the grounds of domestic law or international obligations is like fighting against a naked tyrant by threatening to remove his clothes. The argument that some law, somewhere, should apply to everyone everywhere, seems to spring from an anxious need that everybody everywhere ought to be able to call the police or their lawyer. The legal and humanitarian objections to Guantanamo are valid and necessary, but valid only within their own terms, within the terms that the law actually *is*, that it eternally *is*, and that it *is* everywhere. In so doing, these objections misunderstand what kind of thing the law really is, but it is a misunderstanding that is inherent to the law itself, to the legal and humanitarian understanding of the law's sovereignty.

In fact the law has never been only a legitimate and ultimately binding democratic agreement amongst a bordered people. The law is what commences with the border, what commences with the commencement of sovereignty. The law begins with the sovereign, with the same impossible beginning that institutes the group and the sovereignty of the group. The constituting of the border can only be validated retrospectively, by pointing to the *fact* of the group that exists within that border. So too law is never a merely "juridical" realm, severed from questions of fact. The law relies on fact, on retrospectively established fact, for instance on the *fact* of the promulgation of the Constitution. All law in the end relies on a factual basis, even if this is an impossible and fabulous factual basis. If it does not in the end rely on the final authoring authority of God, law relies on the sovereignty of the event of the Constitution. The founding event, the constituting of the Constitution, is a fundamental and impossible mixture of right and fact. That the Constitution is promulgated is a matter of fact and a matter of an ultimate good, even if it is never possible to be sure of this fact and this good at the moment of inception.

The figure of the sovereign is the embodiment of this mixture of fact and right. Whether monarch or president, the sovereign is never in an ordinary position in relation to law, even if in everyday practice there remains the appearance that the sovereign is not above the law. This difference is marked in the United States in a particularly clear way. The president, like kings of old, retains the right to pardon. That is, he retains the right to suspend the law in special cases and without the necessity of legal reasons. Why does such a right belong to the president? It exists as a recognition of the finitude of the law, a recognition of the possibility that the law makes mistakes. And, more than this, as recognition that the law is only an instrument created at one moment through the promulgation of the Constitution, and refined ever since, but still contingent, imperfect, and limited. The sovereign retains the right to pardon, then, as recognition of the possible necessity that the functioning of law will be in need of correction, a correction that everyday law "itself" remains incapable of.

The idea that lies behind the justification of the Guantanamo camps is the inverse of this right to pardon. The right to pardon is the right to suspend the law because the law is only finite. It exists as a material correction to the limits of instituted law. That the president refers to his common law rights to establish a camp on Cuba finds its possibility in the thought that, over and beyond what the law states, the *real and true meaning* of law is as protection of the people. It is the right and the prerogative of the sovereign to act for that protection. The people in question are not any or everybody but the citizens of the United States. The president is obligated to ensure their protection.

In everyday situations this can only be done by allowing the law to operate in its usual manner. In the extraordinary situation this will not suffice. The common law right to act is based then in the notion that the United States is in an extraordinary situation in relation to the material protection of its citizens. In that extraordinary situation, the argument goes, it is not only possible but necessary that the president act in a manner not limited by legal dogma. The sovereign must ensure the protection of its people, the protection of the possibility of the continuance of law, over and beyond that law itself. The right and indeed the responsibility of the president to act in such a manner is thus bound up with an assessment of the facts of the situation itself.

The point is that the one charged with deciding about the assessment of the situation is the sovereign, the president. The law, in its everyday functioning, does not adapt itself to changing circumstances, except through the long, slow process of the evolution of common law and of constitutional interpretation. What quotidian law cannot admit is the possibility of its own insufficiency in relation to a dramatic alteration in circumstances. Or, rather, it admits this insofar as it is permissible to speak, as the president does, of the common law prerogative of the president to act in relation to the extreme situation.

The president is thus both a member of the group to whom the law applies, and yet stands outside this group, as the one charged with the responsibilities of guarantor of the functioning of the system. The camp, part of American territory by lease, excised from American sovereignty by decision of the president, is the obverse of the sovereign. The enemy combatants are, like the president himself, outside all quotidian law. They are reduced to bodies without rights, whose existence is perpetuated only by the grace of the sovereign. Beyond any notion of transcendental rights and law, they are the *demonstration*, the proof, of the true nature of law in its tie to sovereignty and to the figure of the sovereign.

Sovereignty and security

The philosopher Giorgio Agamben argues that the camp, and the camp inmate, represent the very paradigm of modern sovereignty. Agamben cites the opening line of *Political Theology*, the great work of legal philosophy published by Carl Schmitt in 1922: "Sovereign is he who decides on the exception."[3] This thought expresses the relationship between sovereignty and decision. The law begins with a decision, and the sovereign is the figure who embodies this contingent beginning by reserving the right to decide on the law's suspension in the state of emergency, the "exception." Perhaps it is not even a matter of the sovereign's right, but rather a matter of fact. The law begins, it is born, and as such it contains the mortal possibility of ending or being suspended. The sovereign is the one who holds this possibility, which may perhaps only be revealed retrospectively, when he or she brings an epoch of law to its close. The possibility of deciding that the law will from this moment be suspended is what tells us who, really, the sovereign is. At a more ordinary legal level, the *position* of sovereign is that figure within the law who retains the capacity to decide on the state of emergency that suspends the functioning of ordinary law. The sovereign is the one given the possibility of assessing a situation and making a decision about that situation.

As Agamben shows, the camp is the place that is the material and spatial embodiment of this definition of the sovereign. As the place in which no ordinary law applies, it is outside all territorial jurisdiction while remaining a place within the control of the sovereign.

The order of law and the place of law are separated, and the nature of law as the sovereign decision on right and fact is exposed in the camp:

> The camp is thus the structure in which the state of exception – the possibility of deciding on which is founded sovereign power – is realized *normally*. The sovereign no longer limits himself, as he did in the spirit of the Weimar constitution, to deciding on the exception on the basis of recognizing a given factual situation (danger to public safety): laying bare the inner structure of the ban that characterizes his power, he now de facto produces the situation as a consequence of his decision on the exception. This is why in the camp the *quaestio iuris* is, if we look carefully, no longer strictly distinguishable from the *quaestio facti*, and in this sense every question concerning the legality or illegality of what happened there simply makes no sense. *The camp is a hybrid of law and fact in which the two terms have become indistinguishable.*[4]

In the camp, persons are separated from law and politics, such that they are merely "lives" to be managed. Stripped of rights, the inhabitants are returned to being "mere" human beings, who may be killed or "treated" in any manner, without questions of "human dignity" or the "sacredness" of life ever arising. The question of the legality of what occurs in the camp simply makes no sense. Agamben is drawing upon Walter Benjamin's critical transformation of Schmitt's formulation. For Benjamin, "the 'state of emergency' in which we live is not the exception but the rule."[5] Benjamin is writing in Paris in 1940, shortly before the Nazi apocalypse closed in around him. It was certainly a time at which the state of emergency had the appearance of a norm. The meaning of this statement for Agamben, however, is not limited to the specific context of World War II. Rather, the history of sovereignty is the history of the separation of right and fact, and the camp represents the re-converging of these concepts.

In the camp, right and fact again become one. It is the place that embodies that permanent state of exception by which Benjamin characterized our age. The camp in Guantanamo may in many ways be a less extreme version of the camps created under Hitler. But the fact that the camps are largely accepted by the American public without too much fuss or trouble also tells us something. What had to remain secret in Germany – even if it was the kind of secret that consists in not speaking of something that is nevertheless widely suspected or even known – can at the beginning of the 21st century be organized and implemented in a more or less open fashion.

The true meaning of the War on Terror is that the sovereign, the president, has made the decision to implement the state of exception as the norm. This sounds like an overstatement, if one remembers that the ordinary ways of law continue for the most part to function. Taken in isolation, the camps in Guantanamo remain the exception to this ordinary functioning. Yet it is the *intention* of the Administration to be able to designate as enemy combatants even American citizens "captured" on American soil. Thus it is a mistake to take these camps in isolation from the other paraphernalia of the War on Terror. This includes all those fundamental changes to the understanding of legal rights that come with those Acts concerned with "homeland security." Whether it is the right to imprison without charge or whether it is the use of biometric techniques for the surveillance of the population at large, there is a transformation of the understanding of the relation of citizen to state.

What is involved is a stripping back of rights, but this must be understood correctly. It is not simply the growth of authoritarian law, even though it is this too. Rather, what is occurring is the reduction of the citizen to a mere life, whether it is being controlled by the state or protected. In fact, control and protection converge, as the citizenry gives up the notion that the sovereign is instituted by the people, and the properly Hobbesian sovereign emerges, to whom the citizenry has given up its very right to life on the grounds of the greater security and protection of the Leviathan.

The currently evolving transformation of American foreign policy is part of the same movement toward the state of emergency as the normal state. The notion of pre-emptive military action only makes sense as a necessity prompted by an extreme state of affairs. In this new situation ordinary diplomacy and ordinary notions of the desirability of avoiding war may be sacrificed. The War on Terror is the name given to this state of affairs, in which the entire world is potentially an enemy, potentially able to unleash mass destruction and annihilation.

Faced with such possibilities, the sovereign has a prerogative and is obliged to act pre-emptively. In fact, the logic of "pre-emption" is at the heart not only of American foreign policy, but of "homeland security" and the Guantanamo camps. The fundamental tenet of this logic is that the *situation demands* that the law can no longer operate on the basis that it *responds* to criminal acts. Because the threat is so great, the law must be transformed, such that it acts prior to the carrying out of (terrorist) crimes, and apprehends those who *would have been guilty* in the future. Law is thereby given a martial tenor. It is with this sovereign thought that the state of exception is made the norm. American rhetoric and action are, more clearly and resolutely than during the Cold War, geared toward the notion of perpetual war.

It is tempting to give the name "fascism" to such rhetoric and such forms of governance. It was fascism and the fight against it that was in the mind of Walter Benjamin in 1940. Benjamin expressed disdain for those who felt shock that "such things" could still occur in the middle of the twentieth century, and the same sentiment holds today. Perhaps, however, an entirely new name, yet to be found, would be more appropriate for this conception of the role of government in the common struggle for survival.

What has been demonstrated by Guantanamo is the possibility for the reconciliation of the logic of the camps on the one hand, and the mediated spectacle of democracy that governs the United States on the other hand. We should be neither shocked nor surprised that such a reconciliation could occur. What is occurring in the Cuban camps to enemy combatants of foreign lands mirrors what is occurring in the homeland. And that is the transformation of the conception of the people as the inaugurators and the embodiment of politics and law, bearing rights and freedoms, to a conception of the public as *acted upon* by a governmental machine preoccupied with protection and security. With this preoccupation the very concept of sovereignty may in the end be sacrificed in favor of the security of the situation itself. Beyond sovereignty, beyond law, the eventual outcome of the logic of security is just the concern with the situation itself. Security without even the need for the notion of sovereignty: the global camp.

Afterword: The Politics of Torture

At stake in this case is nothing less than the essence of a free society. Even more important than the method of selecting the people's rulers and their successors is the character of the constraints imposed on the Executive by the rule of law. Unconstrained Executive detention for the purpose of investigating and preventing subversive activity is the hallmark of the Star Chamber.   *Justice John Paul Stevens*[1]

In order to respect the President's inherent constitutional authority to manage a military campaign, 18 USC § 2340A (the prohibition against torture) must be construed as inapplicable to interrogations undertaken pursuant to his Commander-in-Chief authority. Congress lacks authority under Article I to set the terms and conditions under which the President may exercise his authority as Commander-in-Chief to control the conduct of operations during a war. The President's power to detain and interrogate enemy combatants arises out of his constitutional authority as Commander-in-Chief.   *Working Group Report on Detainee Interrogations in the Global War on Terrorism*[2]

Violent Democracy is concerned with the thought that the very idea of democracy is violent. It argues that the concepts of a people, a border, and of foundation are violent *in themselves*, in that they are all ideas that must be *imposed*, in spite of their impossibility, in order to get democracy going. Democracy, if democracy happens, always happens as the assertion of its own existence. And this assertion, because it *is* an assertion, a *self*-assertion, is always threatened, subject to exposure as an apparition. Against this there is no recourse but re-assertion. How better to do this than through the struggle against an enemy – the other against whom a "people" may define itself? Hence some feel that Saddam Hussein was designated the enemy of the United States simply to produce a new enemy, a focal point for the struggle through which America can re-assert *to itself* the strength and solidity of its existence.

In Iraq the latest scene of this assertion is supposedly underway. Reports of 17 July 2004 in the Australian Fairfax media state that to demonstrate the resolve of the incoming government Iyad Allawi, days prior to his appointment as interim Prime Minister, executed several prisoners by his own hand. If these reports are true, the violence of foundation is once again being made manifest in an utterly concrete way. But the entirety of the circumstances surrounding Iraq since the invasion are demonstration enough that those who eagerly proclaim the coming Iraqi democratic republic are fully prepared to accept the violence necessary to inaugurate the new.

In the United States the violence of democracy is being played out in the struggle for the future of those designated enemy combatants. It has an analog in the Australian struggle over the future of the *Tampa* rescuees, described in Chapter Five. Both battles are conducted simultaneously in two arenas – in the contending of ideas that takes place in court, and in physical space, through the violence of imprisonment and confinement. The contest is argued in terms of the relative values of security and freedom, but what is at stake transcends this argument. It is a matter of a sovereign prerogative to act in defense of the people, and a right to act *freely* in circumstances of national peril. In question is who decides when circumstances are exceptional, and what consequences follow from that decision for the future capacity of law to constrain executive action.

Between the United States and Iraq, however, something else is occurring. Both nations, both peoples, are now so intertwined with one another that no easy separation is foreseeable. More than that, the way in which each sees itself, the way in which each unfolds itself, is tied to the other. The being of each *is* in its relation to the other, in the language they unfold together. If this sounds like a vague or faintly mystical proposition, it should be remembered that this connection does not rule out discord any more than it implies harmony. It is in the antagonistic or friendly communication between individuals, and in the communication that takes place through the global systems of information transmission, that each of these nations unfolds its own violent and tortured experience of the other and itself.

Handover

Violent Democracy was written prior to what has become known as the "handover of sovereignty" from the authority set up by the United States military forces to the Iraqi interim government. This handover was conducted in a highly secure and clandestine signing ceremony brought forward by three days, attended by very few Iraqis, and utterly formal. Much about what has changed in the Bush Administration outlook on Iraq since the fall of Baghdad is revealed in the character of this ceremony. Rather than a patriotic and heroic celebration of the birth of a new sovereignty out of the ashes of the former government, the imperatives dictating the form of the handover ritual were security and brevity. The judgment had clearly been made that taking "control" over Iraq with a stroke of Paul Bremer's pen was not the moment to forge the legitimacy, that is, the sacredness, of a new regime of Iraqi law. To emphasize the moment was to risk stamping into the minds of Iraqis the fact that this new sovereignty was granted *to* them or foisted *upon* them by an invading force that not only remains in Iraq, but remains as the dominant power.

The new Iraq was thus founded in an operation that was both mechanical and essentially closed to the Iraqi populace. The conjoined forces of the Administration and the American media had created a narrative in which this handover was one of the culminating events in the fable of the new Iraq. Yet from the epic toppling of Saddam's statue (itself notable for the presence of American military machinery and the absence of the Iraqi public), the crucible of Iraqi sovereignty had been transformed into a mere legal detail, devoid of sentiment. The foremost practical imperative was clearly to spirit Bremer out of Iraq before anything disruptive could occur.

Whether the form of the founding moment of this new Iraq will have consequences for its future remains to be seen. It reflected two things about the present: the decision that what was needed was the *immediate appearance* of Iraqi sovereignty; and the material fact of continuing American military domination. This is not to denounce the event as a meaningless fiction or an orchestrated deception. But what also must not be denied is the degree to which the ways and means of inaugurating this sovereignty were determined by an external power, and equally the degree to which this "sovereignty" *remains* dependent upon and under the influence of the United States.

An official sovereign may be merely an artifice concealing the effective power. This was what Carl Schmitt was referring to in his formulation, cited in Chapter Six, that the true sovereign is the one with the capacity to decide to suspend the law due to exceptional circumstances. In contemporary Iraq, it remains clear where this capacity lies.

The fable of the new Iraq is an old story: the tale of the birth of democracy from out of the defeat of the tyrant. The exigencies of this fable are perhaps responsible for the swiftness with which the "handover of sovereignty" was followed by its sequel, the handover of the tyrant, Saddam Hussein. This ceremony was undoubtedly more peculiar than the preceding one. It was televised but not exactly live, censored yet still revealing. The presiding "judge" seemed himself unsure of the legal status of the occasion, whether it was a simple matter of taking custody of a prisoner, or something like a preliminary hearing en route to a trial.

Saddam was informed of the charges for which he was being held, to which his immediate response was to ask about the grounds of the law under which he was being charged. Was this Iraqi law, or law derived from the American occupation? The equivocation of the judge undoubtedly derived from the fact that one edict *of* the Coalition Provisional Authority was that pre-invasion Iraqi law remained in force, insofar as and precisely to the extent that this law did not contradict the goals of that Authority.

Among the crimes with which Saddam was charged was that of prosecuting the invasion of Kuwait, the precipitative event of the first Gulf War. To this particular charge the prisoner chose immediately to begin his defense. What was the essence of this defense? It was not an argument on the facts but on the law. If, as the judge eventually settled on, his authority as judge derived from pre-existing

Iraqi law, then this law, the old Constitution of Iraq, guaranteed that the President is immune from prosecution for wars conducted in the defense of the Iraqi republic. And, indeed, Article 40 of the Iraqi constitution that was in force prior to the invasion appears to grant this immunity to the President. As Commander-in-Chief of the Iraqi military, Saddam Hussein was in essence saying, he must have a free hand in the conduct of military campaigns, unconstrained by the risk of future legal consequences.

Return of the law

This is not the place to weigh such legal claims in relation to Iraqi law. What is notable, however, is that such arguments directly echo those of the White House in relation to *its* military campaigns in Afghanistan and Iraq. This argument is extended, furthermore, beyond the actual prosecution of the wars as such, to the Administration's right to indefinitely imprison enemy combatants on whatever terms it decides. And, as the *Working Group Report* cited above indicates, the same argument is used to free from all legal constraint those who, in the name of the Commander-in-Chief, are responsible for the treatment, interrogation, and even torture of such enemy combatants. Executive privilege, or indeed a *prerogative* in wartime to act in the best interests of the security of the nation, is thereby interpreted with a breadth that undoes the coherence of the very concept of the rule of law.

In spite of the best efforts of the Administration to classify and conceal, there is now a substantial paper trail indicating the labor expended on the legal questions surrounding detention and interrogation in the exceptional circumstances of the War on Terror. A series of memoranda and reports have become public asking whether and how international treaties and conventions, and domestic law, apply to those designated enemy combatants. We should be clear about the significance of this paper trail. Apologists construe it as merely a matter of obtaining counsel about the legal facts of the situation, about which forms of treatment are legally impermissible. But the real purpose of this legal labor was to find avenues of justification for maintaining imprisonment, and avenues of justification to *facilitate* the harsh treatment of those imprisoned. The real purpose was to circumvent potential legal obstacles to imprisonment and torture.

This is made most explicit in the findings of the *Working Group Report* that the prohibition against torture is inapplicable to actions undertaken as part of the president's authority as Commander-in-Chief. Such a finding is intended to claim that there is no limit to what is legally possible so long as no ceasefire is declared in the War on Terror. Without limits in what it can do, the Administration believes that there ought not be any legal recourse either for those it holds in the course of this war, a war it has itself stated may take generations to resolve.

Of course, all of the labor expended in promoting and justifying this view does not equate to judicial acceptance. Almost simultaneously with the handover of sovereignty in Iraq came a series of judgments in the United States Supreme Court in relation to the legal status of enemy combatants. These cases were essentially to do with appeals for *habeas* relief on behalf of detainees held for two years either in Guantanamo Bay or, if they were American citizens, in military detention in the United States. The decisions in these three cases brought into serious question the claim of the Administration that its actions were beyond legal challenge.

Rumsfeld v Padilla

Rumsfeld v Padilla is the case of Jose Padilla, a man initially arrested in May 2002 as a witness in relation to the attacks of 11 September 2001. Before the warrant could be challenged in court, however, Padilla was designated an enemy combatant and shifted to a South Carolina naval brig. The majority opinion in the case supported the Administration argument that the original *habeas* claim was made in a court without proper jurisdiction to hear the case. The dissenting opinion of Justice Stevens, however, supported by three other justices, was scathing about the methods of the Bush Administration and their implications for American society.

Justice Stevens argued that even more important to the character of a society than the method of determining its ruler are the constraints imposed upon that ruler. In other words, the *limits* imposed upon the sovereign's power are more important to the nature of that society than is the question of whether the sovereign becomes so through democratic process. A democratically elected sovereign unchecked by the rule of law, he implies, is more dangerous to its citizens than a non-democratic ruler who remains bound by an effective legal system.

Justice Stevens takes note that the Administration has conceded that its concern with Padilla was not a matter of law enforcement, nor punishment *as* a terrorist, but rather to find out what he knows *about* terrorism. What was at stake in the case, then, is the right of the government to use "incommunicado detention" for two years as a method of procuring information. Stevens, and the three justices who concur with him, are unequivocal: "Whether the information so procured is more or less reliable than that acquired by more extreme forms of torture is of no consequence."[3] The Bush Administration is in the business of acquiring information through imprisonment used as a tool of torture, and in claiming the right to do so is placing at risk the character of American society.

Rasul v Bush

Rasul v Bush involved two Australian citizens (David Hicks and Mamdouh Habib) and twelve Kuwaiti citizens held thus far for over two years at Guantanamo Bay. The two Australians, it must be said, have been sacrificed on the altar of political expediency by *all* major political parties in Australia. It has been left to private supporters and advocates to intervene on their behalf and to challenge the absolute consignment to oblivion that the Bush Administration preferred. Without such intervention this may well have occurred, as indeed it appears to for the hundreds of detainees about which the future is *utterly* obscure.

In *Rasul v Bush*, Justice Stevens was in the position of offering the majority opinion. In this case the Court decisively rejected the argument that the peculiar status of Guantanamo Bay amounted to anything other than American sovereignty over the territory. The majority rejected outright the claim of the Administration that those held at Guantanamo have no right to a legal hearing. The dissenting justices, on the other hand, concluded simply that no jurisdiction exists where Guantanamo detainees can properly file their *habeas* claim.

Between these two positions fell the concurring opinion of Justice Anthony Kennedy. He admitted the existence of "a realm of political authority over military affairs where the judicial power may not enter."[4] For Justice Kennedy it was a matter of defining the *boundary* between the realm into which the judicial power may enter, and that realm from which it is prohibited from entering on the grounds that the operation of military affairs must be free from judicial interference. Justice Kennedy concurred with the ruling of the majority, on the grounds that the detainees are being held on effectively American territory, and that there must be a jurisdiction in which they can contest their detention.

Justice Kennedy further considered the Administration argument that the urgency of military affairs requires the ability to act unfettered by judicial process. If such an argument is valid, he found, in this case it is inapplicable due to the lengthy and indefinite nature of the detention, far removed from battlefield considerations. For Justice Kennedy, as for the dissenting justices, the right to a legal hearing is not absolute, but conditional, and it is only the extreme form of the assertion of the right to indefinite executive detention on sovereign soil to which he definitively objected.

Hamdi v Rumsfeld

Hamdi v Rumsfeld involves Yaser Esam Hamdi, an American citizen captured by the Northern Alliance during the invasion of Afghanistan. At some point he was turned over to the United States military and, like Padilla, has spent the last two years and more in a South Carolina naval brig. As in the other two cases, Hamdi appealed to the Supreme Court against the legality of this detention.

Once again in this case, the spread of judicial opinion did not only indicate a struggle between the executive and the judiciary. Nor was it merely a division between those justices favorable to Administration objectives and those opposing these objectives. The way in which the Supreme Court responded showed rather a subtle blend of objection to specific claims, but a *tendency* toward acceptance of the most crucial and basic claim of the Administration, that exceptional circumstances legitimate extraordinary measures.

There was not a majority decision in *Hamdi v Rumsfeld* but rather a confluence of opinion between justices not fully in agreement with one another. The main opinion was given by Justice Sandra Day O'Connor, joined by two others. An opinion dissenting in part and agreeing in part was given by Justice David Souter, joined by Justice Ruth Ginsburg. Although disagreeing in its interpretation of the legal situation, this opinion joined with O'Connor in terms of remedy. Between these two opinions the majority was formed.

After 11 September 2001 Congress passed a resolution known as the Authorization for Use of Military Force (AUMF), empowering the President to "use all necessary and appropriate force" in his response to the attacks, on which basis the assault on Afghanistan was authorized. The question for Justice O'Connor was whether the AUMF thereby made legal the subsequent detention of Hamdi. Justice O'Connor rejected the "most extreme rendition" of the Administration's position, that the separation of powers and the nature of the ongoing War on Terror demanded that the Court utterly refrain from interference. She and the supporting justices concluded that a "citizen-detainee" must have the right to challenge their detention, and thus that some kind of civil proceeding must be made available to Hamdi in which this challenge could be heard.

That said, Justice O'Connor recognized that "the exigencies of the circumstances" – that is, the fact that the detainee has been designated an enemy combatant during the ongoing War on Terror – mean that ordinary legal protections may have to be suspended. Hearsay evidence may need to be accepted, for example, and the burden of proof may need to be reversed.[5] Rather than the Administration being obligated to prove that Hamdi is indeed an enemy combatant, it may simply provide hearsay assertions to that effect, which Hamdi must persuasively rebut if he wishes to end his ongoing detention. Thus, even though this case in some ways thwarted the position of the Administration, the most important opinion offered endorsed the detaining of citizens indefinitely on the basis of the AUMF and the denial of ordinary legal protections to those designated as enemy combatants.

That said, not all the justices agreed with this position, and even the opinion of Justice Souter, which joined with O'Connor's to form the plurality, substantially disagreed on the legal situation. Justice Souter in fact did not at all agree that the right to detain had been proven, nor did he agree that the protections of ordinary legal process should be in part suspended due to the nature of the circumstances. It was only for the practical purposes of affording to Hamdi the possibility of challenging his current imprisonment that Justices Souter and Ginsburg agreed to the decision of Justice O'Connor and her supporters.

For Justice Clarence Thomas things were simple. In times of war and national emergency the Administration must not be hampered in the execution of its vital duties, and therefore Hamdi has no right to challenge his detention. Justice Thomas is thus the sole judge to swallow whole the reasoning of the Administration, and he appears ready to sacrifice the very rule of law in the name of the right to prosecute military affairs without fetters.

More interesting is the other dissenting opinion, not least because of the alliance it presents between its author, Justice Antonin Scalia, and its supporter, Justice Stevens. The latter of these is the justice who in *Rumsfeld v Padilla* described Padilla's indefinite detention as a form of torture. The former, Justice Scalia, has frequently been taken to be close to the Administration and in particular its Vice President. Yet the opinion of Justice Scalia in *Hamdi v Rumsfeld* is both supported by Justice Stevens and diametrically opposed to that of Justice Thomas.

What unites these two justices, despite possible political differences, is the thought that a critical purpose of law is the protection of personal liberty against the possibility of tyranny. For Justice Scalia, a writ of *habeas corpus* is not a call for the court to *determine* the nature and type of proceedings in which to challenge detention. It *is* the challenge to that detention, the request that a court find for or against the legality *of* that detention. If the legal basis of detention does not exist, it is not up to judges to search for a basis, nor to invent a mechanism for determining a prisoner's status. Rather, the detainee ought simply be released. Whether this release is for good or ill is a political question, to be determined politically, or else by bringing criminal charges that will permit re-arrest.

The plurality opinion, Justice Scalia argues, represents an attempt to "make everything come out right," rather than simply deciding the question at issue.[6] But whether circumstances are exceptional, or whether the security of the nation demands extraordinary measures are not questions for the judiciary. Whereas Justice O'Connor argued for some flexibility of law due to the ongoing War on Terror, Justice Scalia argues the reverse: the fact that the state of war constantly *tempts* government to curtail liberty should provoke judicial *caution*. That war is declared should not induce pragmatic invention from judges, but rather should be the very moment they are reminded that law does not exist merely to facilitate the executive. It is *particularly* at such times that the judiciary should hold firm to the protections afforded by the Constitution. Law is not merely a tool to serve the ends of government, but the self-standing structure that facilitates democratic process not only by what it enables but equally by what it prevents.

In the name of law and freedom, then, Justices Scalia and Stevens were joined against both the Administration and the plurality opinion of the Supreme Court. What is remarkable is that Scalia's opinion is grounded in a conservatism that prohibits judicial interference in political matters. Not only does Scalia reject the Administration position, but his aversion to judicial involvement in politics means that he also rejects any attempt to weigh or balance the claims of the imprisoned against the claims of the government. Where there is not the legal right to detain, the Court cannot invent new procedures, but must instead order release. Yet this represents only two out of seven justices. The plurality was prepared to sacrifice some of that liberty and some of the law for the sake of the exceptional circumstances currently claimed by the executive. And not only some of the law, but its heart: the meaning of *habeas corpus*, the concept of evidence, and the presumption of innocence.

These three cases were indeed a blow to the attempts of the Bush Administration to avoid any legal accountability whatsoever for its actions in relation to those imprisoned as part of the endless War on Terror. In spite of this, however, what these cases also reveal is that the Supreme Court of the United States is itself participating in that slippage of juridical concepts that permits them to interpret away the foundations of democratic law. On the one hand these decisions represent hope for the detainees of Guantanamo and South Carolina. Yet on the other hand they expose a new preparedness for violence, not only among political leaders, but also in the being of the democratic body politic itself. This movement of outlook transcends opposing political positions, and should be understood not as the property of George W Bush, but as discernible even among many of those who imagine themselves opposing the objectives of the president.

Abu Ghraib

Before the handover of sovereignty, before the Supreme Court rulings on detainees, the single most critical event of the occupation of Iraq was the eruption of the "scandal" over treatment of prisoners at Abu Ghraib. The bad faith in relation to this scandal cannot be overestimated. Almost all of those professing "shock" at this "outrage" are guilty of this bad faith, whether or not this is conscious. For supporters of the American occupation in Iraq the expression of this shock was mandated by political expediency, and the impossibility of admitting publicly that in the pursuit of difficult objectives dirty hands are expected. For opponents the bad faith was just as transparent, for the images of the prisoners were seized upon as a political opportunity, a chance to "prove" the injustice of the occupation.

Despite the many professions of shock, far fewer people would actually have been surprised. More to the point, where there was surprise this needs to be properly understood. It is not surprise that such things could happen, or could be perpetrated by American soldiers. The surprise is more like discomfort at being confronted with what one *would have been prepared to accept oneself*, so long as it remained invisible. It is equivalent to the shock felt by passionate carnivores when confronted with a documentary exposing the treatment of livestock in modern agriculture and its slaughterhouses. The *impact* is real, yet nothing has been shown that was not already (rationally) known. Furthermore, this impact may not impede enjoyment of a fine steak. "I can't believe how they treat those poor animals. Pass the mustard."

Many of the things alleged to have occurred at Abu Ghraib prison are probably frequent occurrences, not only for military prisoners in other circumstances, but in domestic prisons in the United States and throughout the world. That staff at the prison were drawn from correctional facilities in America is indicative that those doing the hiring knew where to find the right personalities for the job. And the fact that Major General Geoffrey D Miller, the officer in charge of interrogations at Guantanamo Bay, was brought to Abu Ghraib to improve the "quality" of the information acquired, is equally significant. It suggests not only that the intention was to enforce a harsher regime at the prison, but also that the circumstances for detainees at Guantanamo were and perhaps are equally unpleasant.

For all the bad faith involved in the reaction to this scandal, the impact is real. It is, to use another analogy, like the Rodney King case that precipitated the Los Angeles riots. The reality that police officers may frequently and even systematically disregard the laws they supposedly enforce may be widely known, and cynicism about the judicial process may be widespread. Perhaps the Los Angeles riots were *not* a genuine political response to the outcome of the Rodney King case, but rather an opportunity seized for engaging in the pleasures of general mayhem. However that stands, without the public transmission of the *images* of King's treatment, not only may the officers involved have escaped legal consequences, but even if somehow they *were* charged, the story would barely have constituted news.

There were British and American newspaper reports of ill treatment by United States military forces in Iraq long before the Abu Ghraib story broke. These included claims of prisoners forced to hold painful positions for long periods, sleep deprivation, kicking and beating, the refusal of painkilling medication to a shot prisoner unless he agreed to cooperate, subjection to extreme cold, as well as cases of prisoners being "rendered" to the security services of nations with a more casual attitude toward torture. But in spite of such reports, the impact of the Abu Ghraib story was incomparably greater than anything that preceded it.

In other words, what was crucial to the significance of Abu Ghraib was not only *what* was alleged to have been done, but *more* importantly its being captured in images and the subsequent distribution of these images in the United States, in Arab countries, and worldwide. Understanding the significance of the event means understanding what happens with the dissemination of such images on such a scale. What does it mean when, through the intervention of the mass media, private communication between torturer and victim is thrust into *our* common experience, our history?

Torture

What is torture?[7] It is not merely one person inflicting pain upon another. If I shoot and thereby wound someone in battle, from a legal standpoint this is explicitly *not* torture, even if my *intention* is to cause suffering rather than death. The ordinary conduct of war is exempt from being treated as torture. One could argue that the entire legal discourse on torture is to assert and establish this boundary, less to prevent torture than to make war permissible.

Torture is thereby caught in all the contradictions involved in the very idea of the "laws of war." However many people were murdered or maimed in the invasion of Iraq, so long as this invasion is deemed to be legal (a perhaps dubious proposition in its own terms, but one unlikely to be tested in court), the number of victims is more or less incidental. But the torture of a single individual is strictly illegal in any circumstances (the Administration claim of the inapplicability of the prohibition notwithstanding). The attempts by the Bush Administration to define torture out of existence are, more than anything else, an attempt to re-define the battlefield of the War on Terror as wide enough to include Abu Ghraib and Guantanamo if not the whole world, and thereby to define what occurs in such places as merely the legally permissible work of war.

From a legal standpoint the definition of torture is not independent of the circumstances in which pain is inflicted. Torture is not an end in itself. Rather, it is conduct perpetrated against somebody for another end, for the end of acquiring information or exacting compliance with some other demand. What makes torture impermissible is that it is painful conduct imposed on somebody already captured or in custody, either to extract information from them, or to make them understand the necessity of complying with the torturer's wishes. Once captured, once off the battlefield, according to the laws of war, one has rights, and that includes not only the right to be spared suffering, but also the right *not* to communicate with one's captors.

Torture is a form of communication, an *act* of communication that intends to provoke a corresponding communicated *return*. When I torture, I communicate to you that you must speak or act in a certain way, and that if you do speak or act as I demand, I may cease to torture. Torture has the goal of reciprocal communication. A systematic use of torture is a cybernetic operation, an organized system for sending and receiving information. But it is not an abstract form of communication, the simple exchange of packets of meaning. Torture is not a system of communication that leaves those involved in it untouched, as when one computer communicates with another. Rather, it involves its participants in the whole of their being as embodied beings, and it operates through the medium of trauma.

Trauma

In ancient Greek "trauma" means wound. In modern medical terms "trauma" means bodily damage, either external or internal, not necessarily implying the penetration or tearing associated with wounding. But even where there is internal trauma without penetration, as may occur for instance in a car crash, the internal damage is a kind of rupturing or breaking (such that there is, say, internal bleeding).

The concept of trauma has been extended by analogy to apply in psychology, for instance in the syndrome called "post-traumatic stress disorder."

The concept of psychological trauma is sometimes posited on an image of the mind as a bordered object, through the surface of which sensation passes on its way to consciousness. It is imagined that in everyday experience the mind processes and filters perception, the mind's surface functioning as a protective barrier that "copes" with the shock of raw experience by admitting or excluding raw sensation. In psychological *trauma*, however, the magnitude of a particular sensation or experience is too great, causing it to break through the protective psychic "skin" to "flood" consciousness in an uncontrolled way that causes damage. The violence of psychological trauma is thus that of experiences or sensations forcefully penetrating our psychic being in a damaging way. The "flood" of intense raw sensation induces shockwaves that continue to be felt and to affect us long after the experience itself.

Such analogies litter the history of psychological theory, including psychoanalysis. Yet perhaps reducing the process of experience to a familiar physical analogy makes what is peculiar to "psychological" experience more difficult to isolate.

In fact, the concept of mental trauma is better understood differently. When we experience, when we receive sensation, this is *never* "raw" data, but always mediated by the work of interpretation. The first proof is the experience of time itself. Time is not experienced as a succession of present moments but rather as a flow, from the past into the future. In order to hear a single musical note, let alone a melody, we must be able to perceive the continuing presence of this note throughout the course of its being sustained. That this is possible is not just a "natural" reflection of the way things are, but the consequence of the *active* way in which experience is received. This is the lesson of phenomenology.[8]

It is thus not that there is a *barrier*, a mental skin, through which perception passes on its way to consciousness. Rather, there is no experience that does not immediately involve our own perceptual activity, the work of comprehension, selection, assimilation. What is trauma, then, if not the forceful rupturing and penetration of mental skin? The work of perceptual activity consists in *comprehending* experience, in *grasping* experience, either as something familiar, something assimilable to the flow of remembered experience, *or else* as something new or strange. When an unfamiliar experience occurs, something not found in the stock of previous experience stored as memory, such as one's first car crash, a different kind of work must be done by the brain, *accommodating* the new and unfamiliar. This possibility of accepting and grasping new experience is the human capacity for novelty.

Experience that is *traumatic*, then, is not experience that ruptures our protective mental barrier. Rather, it is experience that is so difficult to assimilate that there is a *significant delay* in accommodating the shock of the new. The traumatic event, if it can be accommodated, cannot be accommodated immediately or quickly. The work of comprehending and sorting experience, which ordinarily operates in the course of the experience, continues long after the event.

And thus the traumatic event is finally incorporated as ordinary memory, *if it ever is*, much later than a merely novel experience.

Such an understanding of trauma does not posit traumatic experience as "raw." Every experience involves the work of comprehension. Every experience must be grasped in a particular way as it occurs. If I place a loaded gun at your head, there is the potential for traumatic experience. The awareness of the possibility of imminent death excites the brain, forces it to try and grasp a situation that is not only unfamiliar. You may be forced to *imagine* the imminent possibility of the end of experience, to imagine the unimaginable, to be aware of the immediate possibility of the absolute loss of awareness. But the impossibility of accommodating this means that you may not even comprehend your own perceptions or their significance, and thus the experience may reverberate across your future memory as trauma.

In other words, psychic trauma always involves interpretation. The experience described above depends upon understanding what a gun is and the potential it contains. It is not the raw perception of a gun at one's head that is traumatic, but the perception of the *significance* of that fact. And perhaps the twelfth time one undergoes such an experience, it becomes a dramatic but non-traumatic moment, because the experience, just as potentially fatal, is nevertheless familiar and assimilable. Perhaps.

If I undergo physical torture, involving intense pain, this experience may be very different depending upon the previous course of my life. It is well known that the possibility exists for training the body, through the discipline of repetition, to endure physical extremes, or even not to feel the pain involved in certain situations. Marathon runners, for instance, train their bodies to function in situations where the "ordinary" physical responses of one's body work to halt that functioning. This capacity to *discipline* one's reaction to physical sensation shows that even the experience of physical pain or injury is not raw, but interpreted and grasped in particular ways. The potential for such discipline shows that mind and body are not as distinguishable as the distinction between physical and psychical trauma suggests. The overall perceptual apparatus of the human being, let us say, always works on experience, even where that experience is violent or damaging.

Torture and trauma in Iraq

This brings us back to Abu Ghraib. Torture is a form of communication between torturer and tortured. Trauma is experience that cannot be quickly or easily assimilated to the *stock* of experience gathered in the course of life. What this amounts to is that between torturer and tortured a language is unfolding itself. It is not a language of "equal" partners, obviously. Yet without presupposing the possibility of being understood, torture is impossible. The tortured must see or presume that the gun is loaded for it to function as a sign with the capacity to induce psychic trauma. Torture victims must grasp that the pain they feel is telling them something more than just that their body is suffering. They must understand that something is being demanded of them, for torture to be effective.

But, in that case, torture requires that the *torturer* know the victim well enough to know *how* to be understood. What is evident about Abu Ghraib is the degree to which this fact was understood by the apparent perpetrators. Torture, or the inducement of trauma for the purpose of acquiring information or exacting compliance with some other demand, is not the same for everyone. With this in mind techniques for inducing trauma were devised for Abu Ghraib that were intended to be specific to the victims. The use of techniques of humiliation or degradation, for instance, was clearly done with the thought that for *these* people, for these *Muslims*, such experiences are inassimilable to their understanding and experience of masculinity. The very classification of an experience as degrading or humiliating depends upon one's own experience and history, and on the experience and history of the group of which one is a member, of one's "culture." It may be that many forms of torture are generally and widely, if not universally, applicable, but the point is that effort was expended in the *invention* of techniques based on the thought that *these* people will find *this* experience intolerable.

Another example is the decision to throw a copy of the Koran into a toilet in front of a prisoner. What is remarkable is not that this will mean nothing to one person and may mean everything to another. What is remarkable is the imagination expended in the devising of such a method, and the recognition it involves that what is at stake is the unfolding of a *mutual language*. To devise such a technique does not only involve forcing the victim to comprehend what I am doing. It also involves my effort to understand the language of the victim.

What is unfolded between torturer and victim, the language they (unequally) produce together, then comes to have its own force and momentum, granting to both tortured and torturer a new set of experiences to be assimilated to the stock of their memories. The torturer and the tortured are witnesses to the same private and intimate scene (if from vastly different standpoints), witnesses to the communication and secret knowledge shared between them. In this mutuality torturer and tortured become bound to one another, in spite of themselves, as long as memory lasts. It is as joint witnesses to their shared acts and scenes that both become who they will be in their respective futures.

That is why what is important about the Abu Ghraib scandal is that a private communication becomes part of public experience. Or at least it seems to. We are all witnesses to the images of the events of that prison. But *only* to the images. To the extent that such images are novel to each individual's experience, they require processing and assimilation. To the extent they confirm our past experience they are merely accommodated. But perhaps what makes the Abu Ghraib event significant is the "feeling" we have all jointly witnessed an event. In fact we have not. We have neither experienced nor witnessed an event of torture. Rather, all we have done is *receive* images broadcast on television.

When we experience a photograph or digital image on the television news, every individual receives the identical data. We each receive the image in our own particular way in our own particular stream of experience. But when something is shown for the first time on CNN millions of people jointly and simultaneously seem to experience the same thing in the same way. Each person is witness to the same apparent event. And for each person a new element in the language of his or her experience is imparted. But what is imparted is a new common experience, *not* the language that unfolds between torturer and tortured. We imagine we are placed through our capacity for sympathy (with either or both parties) into this private language, but in fact we remain in the common world of televised experience. We are deceived by the apparatus of technologically communicated experience. We are witnesses to nothing.

Counter-rhythm

Those opposing the occupation of Iraq, opposing it in violent deed, appear aware that the images of Abu Ghraib are insufficient to call the mass of Western individuals to their notion of conscience. For those violently opposing the American presence in Iraq, the images of Abu Ghraib are further proof to the Arab world of the pleasure taken by America in the humiliation of citizens of Arab countries. Some in the West will be troubled, but the secret or not so secret pleasure taken in the other's suffering is common and predictable.

At the same time, those violently opposing the occupation of Iraq are acutely aware that the global communication system holds the potential to engender experiences in a mass of people. And this potential means the possibility to determine the experience, the common history, of entire populations, and thus to influence the future of those populations. The capacity for a tiny group to have this influence is unprecedented, and is being seized upon in a new way in the fight for the future of Iraq.

What does it mean to take a man hostage, to give notice that at a specified time he will be killed, to take a knife at the designated moment and saw his head off, to place the video imagery of this act on the internet, and to have this imagery broadcast on television within hours, in whole or in part, throughout the globe? It does not mean that America will leave Iraq. It does not mean that an Islamic state will emerge in Iraq. And it is not revenge. What does it mean to announce that something will happen, and then to carry out that action in plain view of the public? Is it an attempt to place every individual made aware of this sequence of events into the position of the victim? Or, rather, is it to make every individual who is aware of this situation responsible for it?

When the people of South Korea go to bed one night assured that things are being done to secure the release of their citizen-hostage, and when they awake to find on their screens the hysterical screams of the family of the murdered victim, the goal is for each Korean individual to be placed in a position of responsibility. This does not mean that each will take on that responsibility in the same way or at all. Many may refuse to do so. But by opening up the gap between the announcement of a future horrific homicide and the carrying out of that act, the individual is placed into the temporality of the event, in the same way as one is placed into the temporality of a piece of music.

An experience is thereby produced that is potentially far more powerful than a bomb that kills hundreds. One finds out about a bombing after the fact, and is horrified or not, but it becomes the experience of a *fait accompli*. But the recent beheadings function according to a different logic, with a greater capacity to affect the course of material events, as shown by the response of the Philippines government to this very situation.

Although 11 September 2001 was not announced prior to being carried out, the spectacular success of the event lies in the fact that for so many millions of people it *unfolded* live on television. That is, it was *not* instantaneous like a bombing, but instead took place across time. It was not merely that first one then another plane hit the World Trade Center, or that first one and then the other tower collapsed, with everything that these events implied for the human beings involved. It was also the fact that there seemed to be an indeterminate number of other hijacked planes heading for unknown destinations. For those watching live, the sensation was created that *one did not know* what would happen next, that suddenly anything might happen. One was not simply made aware of an event after the fact, but was living in the time of that more or less traumatic event.

But whereas the events of that day erupted in front of an American population that struggled to find any sense or responsibility in them, the goal of beheading hostages seems to be to communicate to a vast audience in a language intended to be immediately comprehensible. Being placed into the before and after of the event, the individual and the mass is placed into a communication, in the language of the utmost responsibility, for the mortal fate of somebody who could be anybody. Whether such an event is truly traumatic for the mass that experiences it, it seems clear that the world's communication systems are being harnessed to create an experience that *must* be assimilated in one way or another, according to conscience.

But is it not the case that those who subscribe to the most radically violent forms of Islam are motivated, at bottom, by hatred and contempt for modern Western society? This is usually expressed as hatred of "Western values." But what is hated is not particular values, but rather the very idea of values as such. A world where one has this value or that, this preference or that, and more particularly a world where no value is transcendent, where there are *only* values, is antithetical to the idea of religious truth. What is hated is the conjunction of value and desire, where values are a matter of choice, of the value we give them because of the degree to which they conform to the desires we have. To the religious extremist this is a doctrine of sin.

The West is despised because it has produced an immensely powerful system that not only disseminates values, but invents and coordinates individual desire on a mass scale. And this system is the system of mass communication: television, the internet, and so on. It is the system for the transmission of mass advertising, the mass delivery of experience, experience of that which we should desire.[9] And this system for proliferating the desire for consumption naturally proliferates at the same time the adoption of whatever values promote this desire.

At bottom, all religious objections to the contemporary world are rejections of the world as produced by the global system for disseminating experience. This system on the one hand infinitely homogenizes desire, and yet on the other hand is responsible for its infinite relativization. Any particular desire for any particular thing (commodity, experience) is legitimate, and is legitimated by the fact that others are always already succumbing to the very same desire, insofar as they are simultaneously receiving the very same experience on television or the internet. In place of individual responsibility before God there comes the mass market of desire.

Is it not the goal of religious extremists to violently force each to take proper responsibility in the face of God, rather than in the face of what is received in common via systems of communication technology? If their hatred is something more than a reaction to American *deeds* in the Middle East, if it has a meaning that is *in some way* religious, then it is a reaction in favor of each person's religious responsibility. And what is thereby opposed is the destruction of responsibility, a destruction that is the *product* of the system of planetary communication.

And thus the very *effectiveness* of a strategy such as globally broadcast beheading may be its undoing. With such strategies, with such attempts to force the assimilation of a supposedly inassimilable experience, the perpetrators risk missing that on the internet, on television, *in the end* everything is assimilable and nothing is traumatic. Rather than making each one a witness to his or her own responsibility, the individual is able to cope with more and more. The experience of watching video imagery of the beheading of a human being becomes a kind of advertisement, producing its own kind of desire.

This is not the same thing as the false claim that adolescents who watch horror movies become murderers in adulthood. It is that, as an event shared simultaneously by millions together, what occurs is simply the production of the next element in the unfolding language of mass communication. For a moment each individual is placed into the temporality of one person's mortal fate. But it may be that the result is not the creation of witnesses to an execution as much as merely the production of another universal reference point for common experience. And, with this new shared element in our mutual language of *non*-communication, we become by degrees more violent in our capacity to accept, to ignore, to desire, as a people, as a citizenry, that which is received by all together. "Shocking" imagery may produce an immediate reaction, but *in the end* it may do nothing more than *contribute* to that destruction of individual experience and responsibility – the destruction to which the radically and violently religious object. In the end, perhaps, it only adds to the increasingly violent essence of those worlds that proclaim themselves, violently, democratic.

Notes

Introduction

1 Primo Levi, "Afterword: The Author's Answers to His Readers' Questions," *If This is a Man, and The Truce* (London: Penguin, 1979), pp. 396–7.

2 Carl Schmitt, *Political Theology: Four Chapters on the Concept of Sovereignty* (Cambridge, Mass. & London, The MIT Press, 1985), p. 36.

3 Cf., Jacques Derrida, *Politics of Friendship* (London & New York: Verso, 1997), pp. 103–4; cf., Jacques Rancière, *Disagreement: Politics and Philosophy* (Minneapolis & London: University of Minnesota Press, 1999), ch. 2.

4 Giorgio Agamben, *Remnants of Auschwitz: The Witness and the Archive* (New York: Zone Books, 1999), p. 69.

1 The High Horse and the Low Road

1 "Defense Planning Guidance," <http://www.pbs.org/wgbh/pages/frontline/shows/iraq/etc/wolf.html> at 28 July 2004.

2 Winston Churchill, speech in the House of Commons, 11 November 1947, <http://www.digiserve.co.uk/quotations/search.cgi?=Subject+ & terms=politics> at 28 July 2004.

3 Saul Bellow, *Ravelstein* (London: Penguin, 2000), p. 60. Obviously this is not a scholarly source, yet Bellow was a close friend of Bloom, and it is more or less clear that the work is intended to be a "true" account of Bellow's experience of Bloom. It therefore seems reasonable to take "Ravelstein's" remarks about "Gorman" as some kind of evidence. That, at least, is the best rationalization we can offer for adopting what is a useful procedure in this case.

4 Francis Fukuyama, *The End of History and The Last Man* (London: Penguin, 1992).

5 Leo Strauss, *What is Political Philosophy? And Other Studies* (Chicago & London: University of Chicago Press, 1959), p. 55.

6 This is reflected, for instance, in the concise way in which Strauss describes the foundation of the political philosophy of Hobbes: "The rationality of the political teaching consists in its being acceptable to passion, in its being agreeable to passion. The passion that must be the basis of the rational political teaching

is fear of violent death." Leo Strauss, "Niccolo Machiavelli," in Leo Strauss & Joseph Cropsey (eds.), *History of Political Philosophy*, 3rd edn. (Chicago & London: University of Chicago Press, 1987), p. 298.

7 Lars von Trier, *Epidemic* (1988).

8 Even before 11 September George W Bush was thematizing the certainties that were lost and the certainties that remain after the fall of the USSR, as shown by this gem from 2000 (Albuquerque, reported in *The Washington Post*, 31 May 2000): "This is a world that is much more uncertain than the past. In the past we were certain, we were certain that it was us versus the Russians in the past. We were certain, and therefore we had huge nuclear arsenals aimed at each other to keep the peace. That's what we were certain of. [. . .] You see, even though its an uncertain world, we're certain of some things. We're certain that even though the 'evil empire' may have passed, evil still remains."

9 Niccolo Machiavelli, *The Prince* (London: Penguin, 1961), p. 118.

2 Strangers in a Familiar Land

1 Roger Scruton, *The West and the Rest: Globalization and the Terrorist Threat* (London & New York: Continuum, 2002), p. 6.

2 Jean-Pierre Vernant, "Tensions and Ambiguities in Greek Tragedy," in Jean-Pierre Vernant & Pierre Vidal-Naquet, *Myth and Tragedy in Ancient Greece* (New York: Zone Books, 1988), p. 41.

3 Roger Scruton, *The West and the Rest*, p. 149.

4 *Ad hominem* arguments are the enemy of reasoned debate, and hence we will apologise in advance and relegate to a footnote the following: Scruton, it must be said, is very keen on these virtues of Western society. Of course, Scruton is just as concerned with the danger that these virtues may be receding even in the West, due to globalization and other factors which have led to a decline in the sense of territorial (or, more simply, national) loyalty. Nevertheless it is obvious that the West is still today to be distinguished by the presence of these virtues, among them the notion of public spirit, which Scruton describes on page 56: "Public spirit is perhaps the most misunderstood of all the features of citizenship, and the one that has been most precious in Anglophone history. The public-spirited person gives time, energy, and resources for the benefit of others whom he does not know, and with a view to perpetuating the social order of which he is a beneficiary. He is the founder of schools, hospitals, and facilities for the use of those unborn." Doubtless Scruton does not intend to describe himself here. Nevertheless, it is impossible to resist mentioning the "scandal" of a few years ago, when it was discovered that Scruton was being paid £4500 per month by Japan Tobacco, but that he had failed to disclose this to several newspapers who were employing him to write columns. The discovery was made while he was negotiating to increase his remuneration from the Japanese tobacco company. Perhaps Scruton would argue that defending smoking is a matter of defending freedom against the tyranny of political correctness, and was therefore a matter of public spirit. Yet it is difficult to reconcile this thought with the founding

of schools and hospitals, especially at a time when the tobacco industry – the epitome of globalized capitalism that apparently Scruton fears so much – is faced with declining smoking in the West, and hence actively engaged in the promotion of its products amongst the rest.

5 Roger Scruton, *The West and the Rest*, p. 53.
6 *Ibid.*, pp. 11–12.
7 *Ibid.*, p. 60.
8 *Ibid.*, p. 24.
9 *Ibid.*, pp. 12–13.
10 Jacques Derrida, "Declarations of Independence," *Negotiations: Interventions and Interviews, 1971–2001* (Stanford: Stanford University Press, 2002), p. 50.
11 Roger Scruton, *The West and the Rest*, p. 2.
12 Sophocles, *Antigone, The Women of Trachis, Philoctetes, Oedipus at Colonus* (Cambridge, Mass. & London: Harvard University Press, 1994, trans. Hugh Lloyd-Jones), pp. 44–5.
13 Jacques Lacan, *The Ethics of Psychoanalysis* (London: Routledge, 1992), p. 278. Cf., Martin Heidegger, *Hölderlin's Hymn "The Ister"* (Bloomington & Indianapolis: Indiana University Press, 1996), p. 116.
14 Jacques Lacan, *The Ethics of Psychoanalysis*, p. 279.

3 Sorry We Killed You

1 Jacques Derrida, in "On Forgiveness: A Roundtable Discussion with Jacques Derrida," in John D Caputo, Mark Dooley, & Michael J Scanlon (eds.), *Questioning God* (Bloomington & Indianapolis: Indiana University Press, 2001), pp. 56–7.
2 M Night Shyamalan, *The Sixth Sense* (1999).
3 Cf., Jacques Rancière, *Disagreement: Politics and Philosophy* (Minneapolis & London: University of Minnesota Press, 1999).

4 The Great Debate

1 Thomas Mann, *The Magic Mountain* (London: Penguin, 1927), p. 541.
2 William Burroughs, in Christopher Silvester (ed.), *The Penguin Book of Interviews: An Anthology from 1859 to the Present Day* (London: Penguin, 1993), p. 582.

5 Border Protection and Alien Friends

1 Justice Windeyer, in the decision of *Lo Pak* in the Supreme Court of New South Wales, 1888, cited by Chief Justice Black in *Ruddock v Vadarlis*, Australian Law Reports (2001), 183, p. 21.
2 Kim Beazley, cited in David Marr & Marian Wilkinson, *Dark Victory* (Crows Nest: Allen & Unwin, 2003), p. 95.
3 *Ibid.*, p. 125.

4 Justice North, in *VCCL v MIMA*, Australian Law Reports (2001), 182, p. 655.
5 Chief Justice Black, in *Ruddock v Vadarlis*, p. 10.
6 Lord Dunedin, cited by Justice Black in *ibid.*, p. 13.
7 Justice French, in *ibid.*, p. 52.
8 Justice French, in *ibid.*, p. 54.
9 Chief Justice Black, in *ibid.*, p. 24.
10 Justice French, in *ibid.*, p. 57.
11 Justice French, in *ibid.*, pp. 57–8.
12 Justice Beaumont, in *ibid.*, p. 32.
13 David Marr & Marian Wilkinson, *Dark Victory*, p. 163.

6 Enemy Combatants

1 Giorgio Agamben, *Homo Sacer: Sovereign Power and Bare Life* (Stanford: Stanford University Press, 1998), pp. 166–7.
2 Thomas Hobbes, *Leviathan* (Cambridge: Cambridge University Press, 1966, revised student edition), pp. 91–4.
3 Carl Schmitt, *Political Theology: Four Chapters on the Concept of Sovereignty* (Cambridge, Mass. & London: The MIT Press, 1985), p. 5.
4 Giorgio Agamben, *Homo Sacer*, p. 170.
5 Walter Benjamin, "On the Concept of History," *Selected Writings, Volume 4: 1938–1940* (Cambridge, Mass. & London: Belknap Press, 2003), p. 392.

Afterword: The Politics of Torture

1 *Rumsfeld v Padilla* 542 US (Stevens J 11). Note that the method of referencing these cases of the Supreme Court is due to the fact that they are not yet reported in a properly paginated volume.
2 *Working Group Report on Detainee Interrogations in the Global War on Terrorism: Assessment of Legal, Historical, Policy, and Operational Considerations* (6 March 2003), p. 20 (pagination is to the fax-transmission id; it is p. 19 of the on-line pdf doc). This is an internal Pentagon document, available online from the Center for Constitutional Rights, <http://www.ccr-ny.org/v2/reports/docs/PentagonReportMarch.pdf> at 28 July 2004.
3 *Rumsfeld v Padilla* 542 US (Stevens J 11–12).
4 *Rasul et al v Bush* 542 US (Kennedy J 3).
5 *Hamdi v Rumsfeld* 542 US (O'Connor J 26–7).
6 *Hamdi v Rumsfeld* 542 US (Scalia J 24).
7 Article 1, paragraph 1 of the *Convention against Torture and Other Cruel, Inhuman or Degrading Treatment or Punishment* (Geneva: Office of the High Commissioner for Human Rights, 1984) reads as follows: "For the purposes of this Convention, 'torture' means any act by which severe pain or suffering, whether physical or mental, is intentionally inflicted on a person for such purposes as obtaining from him or a third person information or a confession, punishing him for an act he or a third person has committed or is suspected of

having committed, or intimidating or coercing him or a third person, or for any reason based on discrimination of any kind, when such pain or suffering is inflicted by or at the instigation of or with the consent or acquiescence of a public official or other person acting in an official capacity. It does not include pain or suffering arising only from, inherent in or incidental to lawful sanctions."

8 Cf., Bernard Stiegler, *Aimer, s'aimer, nous aimer: Du 11 septembre au 21 avril* (Paris: Galilee, 2003), pp. 39–40. Some of the ideas that follow in this chapter are an adaptation of the ideas expressed in Stiegler's remarkable book.

9 Cf., *ibid.*, p. 22.

References

Agamben, Giorgio, *Homo Sacer: Sovereign Power and Bare Life* (Stanford: Stanford University Press, 1998).

Agamben, Giorgio, *Remnants of Auschwitz: The Witness and the Archive* (New York: Zone Books, 1999).

Bellow, Saul, *Ravelstein* (London: Penguin, 2000).

Benjamin, Walter, *Selected Writings, Volume 4: 1938–1940* (Cambridge, Mass. & London: Belknap Press, 2003).

Black CJ, Beaumont J, & French J, *Ruddock v Vadarlis*, Australian Law Reports (2001), 183: 1–58.

Caputo, John D, Mark Dooley, & Michael J Scanlon (eds.), *Questioning God* (Bloomington & Indianapolis: Indiana University Press, 2001).

Center for Constitutional Rights, *Working Group Report on Detainee Interrogations in the Global War on Terrorism: Assessment of Legal, Historical, Policy and Operational Considerations* (2003), <http://www.ccr-ny.org> at 6 March 2003.

Derrida, Jacques, *Negotiations: Interventions and Interviews, 1971–2001* (Stanford: Stanford University Press, 2002).

Derrida, Jacques, *Politics of Friendship* (London & New York: Verso, 1997).

Fukuyama, Francis, *The End of History and The Last Man* (London: Penguin, 1992).

Heidegger, Martin, *Hölderlin's Hymn "The Ister"* (Bloomington & Indianapolis: Indiana University Press, 1996).

Hobbes, Thomas, *Leviathan* (Cambridge: Cambridge University Press, revised student edn).

Lacan, Jacques, *The Ethics of Psychoanalysis* (London: Routledge, 1992).

Levi, Primo, *If This is a Man, and The Truce* (London: Penguin, 1979).

Machiavelli, Niccolo, *The Prince* (London: Penguin, 1961).

Mann, Thomas, *The Magic Mountain* (London: Penguin, 1927).

Marr, David, & Marian Wilkinson, *Dark Victory* (Crows Nest: Allen & Unwin, 2003).

North J, *VCCL v MIMA*, Australian Law Reports (2001), 182: 617–56.

Office of the High Commissioner for Human Rights, *Convention against Torture and Other Cruel, Inhuman or Degrading Treatment or Punishment* (Geneva: Office of the High Commissioner for Human Rights, 1984).

Rancière, Jacques, *Disagreement: Politics and Philosophy* (Minneapolis & London: University of Minnesota Press, 1999).

Schmitt, Carl, *Political Theology: Four Chapters on the Concept of Sovereignty* (Cambridge, Mass. & London, The MIT Press, 1985).

Scruton, Roger, *The West and the Rest: Globalization and the Terrorist Threat* (London & New York: Continuum, 2002).

Shyamalan, M Night, *The Sixth Sense* (1999).

Silvester, Christopher (ed.), *The Penguin Book of Interviews: An Anthology from 1859 to the Present Day* (London: Penguin, 1993).

Sophocles, *Antigone, The Women of Trachis, Philoctetes, Oedipus at Colonus* (Cambridge, Mass. & London: Harvard University Press, 1994, trans. Hugh Lloyd-Jones).

Stiegler, Bernard, *Aimer, s'aimer, nous aimer: Du 11 Septembre au 21 avril* (Paris: Galilee, 2003).

Strauss, Leo, *What is Political Philosophy? And Other Studies* (Chicago & London: University of Chicago Press, 1959).

Strauss, Leo, & Joseph Cropsey (eds.), *History of Political Philosophy*, 3rd edn. (Chicago & London: University of Chicago Press, 1987).

von Trier, Lars, *Epidemic* (1988).

Vernant, Jean-Pierre, & Pierre Vidal-Naquet, *Myth and Tragedy in Ancient Greece* (New York: Zone Books, 1988).

Index

11 September 2001 12, 18–20, 30–1, 37, 40, 116, 128–30, 137–8, 156, 159, 171

Abbott, Tony 113
Abu Ghraib prison 162–4, 168–70
Afghanistan 23, 39, 40, 128, 130, 138–9
Agamben, Giorgio 11, 124, 146–7
Allawi, Iyad 152
Antigone (Sophocles) 43, 53–8
apologies 67–8, 69, 71–4, 75
Auschwitz 11, 13, 56, 140–1, 143
Auster, Paul 31
Australia 12, 50–1, 59–61, 64–71, 74–8, 81–5, 88–103, 105, 108–23, 128, 157

Beaumont, Justice Bryan 117, 120–1
Beazley, Kim 113, 114–15
Bellow, Saul 27, 174
Benjamin, Walter 147, 149
bin Laden, Osama 129, 130
Black, Chief Justice Michael 117, 118, 120
Bloom, Allan 27, 30, 36
bodies 3–4, 165
borders 7, 32–4, 41–2, 45, 86, 104–5, 107–8, 113, 131–2, 136, 144, 151
Bremer, Paul 153
burial 43, 55–7

Burroughs, William S 81
Bush, George W 14, 23, 30, 35, 41, 129, 162, 174–5

capitalism 1, 11, 18–19, 23, 31, 107–8
chance 29, 30–1
Cheney, Dick 20, 24
Churchill, Winston 26
Cleisthenes 5
Clinton, Bill 14, 40, 71, 128
Cold War, the 17–18, 29, 39–40, 149
concentration camps 13, 74, 124, 125–6, 139, 140–1, 143, 146–8, 149–50
confirmation 8, 50, 51–2, 88–9, 137
Cowen, Zelman 83
crime 52–3, 55–6, 58, 62, 64–7, 75, 78
crimes against humanity 10–11
Cuba 125–8, 141

Dark Victory (Marr & Wilkinson) 115, 122
"Declaration of Independence" 48–50
"Defense Planning Guidance" (Wolfowitz) 20–6
democracy 2–3, 3–8, 11–13, 23–4, 26, 28–9, 39–42, 46–7, 50–1, 52–3, 71, 72–3, 86–9, 93–5, 104–5, 129, 132, 133–6, 151–2
Derrida, Jacques 49, 59

enemy 10, 12, 19, 22, 33–5, 132, 140, 151–2
enemy combatants 129, 140, 141–2, 146, 155–8, 159
Epidemic (von Trier) 31–2
extermination of the Jews 10–11, 27, 29–30, 140–1

fascism 1, 13, 149
forgetting 63–4, 65, 69–70, 78
forgiveness 59, 70–1, 74
fortress 32–4
foundation 7–8, 47–53, 58, 76–7, 86–7, 88–9, 136, 151
freedom of speech 11–12
French, Justice Robert 117, 119–20
Fukuyama, Francis 27

Ginsburg, Justice Ruth 159–60
globalization 11, 12, 13, 18, 107–8, 172–3
Gore, Al 14–15
Greece, ancient 4–5, 43, 131, 138
Guantanamo Bay 25, 127–8, 140–1, 141–4, 145, 147–9, 157–8, 161, 163, 164
Gulf War I (1991) 9, 154–5

Habib, Mamdouh 157–8
Hamdi, Yaser Esam 158–62
Hanson, Pauline 90, 111–13, 114–15
haunting 8, 17, 29, 34–5, 50, 61–4, 66, 75, 76, 77, 78–9
head of state 85–6, 88, 91–6
Heidegger, Martin 54
Hicks, David 157–8
Hitler, Adolf 34, 93, 141, 148
Hobbes, Thomas 15, 24, 133, 142, 148, 174
Hölderlin, Friedrich 17
Hollingworth, Peter 92
Holocaust, *see* extermination of the Jews
house of review 90–1

Howard, John 75, 76, 99–101, 111, 112–13
Hussein, Saddam 152, 154–5
humanitarianism 40–1, 106–7, 142–4

immigration 108–10, 111, 128
imperialism, democratic 25, 39–42
Iraq, invasion of 23–4, 26, 34–5, 36–9, 41–2, 53, 153–5
Israel 28, 90

Keating, Paul 76
Kennedy, Justice Anthony 158
Kerr, John 92–3, 95
King, Rodney 163

Lacan, Jacques 54–6
law 9, 10, 12, 13, 26, 43–4, 46, 53–5, 56–8, 71, 77, 78–9, 87, 97–8, 143–6, 154–62
Leichhardt, Ludwig 82
Levi, Primo 1
liberalism 85–6
Liebknecht, Karl 51

Machiavelli, Niccolo 31, 32–3, 35
Mann, Thomas 80, 82
Marr, David *see Dark Victory*
McKinley, William 125–6
Miller, Major General Geoffrey D 163
miracle 52–3, 58, 64, 67, 75, 78
monarchism 84–5
monarchy 5, 25–6, 95–6, 99
Murray, Les 98–102
Musil, Robert 125

Nader, Ralph 110
National Socialism 5, 27–8, 29–30, 36, 52, 68, 74, 106, 126, 140, 141
Nauru 122
North, Justice Anthony 115–16, 121

O'Connor, Justice Sandra Day
    159–61
One Nation party, see Hanson,
    Pauline

Padilla, Jose 156–7
people, the 5–6, 7, 48–51, 86, 151
populism 110
Powell, Colin 33
preamble, Australian referendum on
    96–103

reconciliation 68–71
religion 43–4, 47–9, 53–5, 94–5, 96,
    99, 172–3
republic, Australian referendum on
    82–5, 96, 103
responsibility 67–8, 172–3
Rinnan, Arne 114, 120, 122
Ruddock, Philip 115
Rumsfeld, Donald 14, 16, 20, 33, 41,
    156
Rwanda 9, 74

Scalia, Justice Antonin 160–2
Scheidemann, Philipp 51
Schmitt, Carl 5, 146, 154
Scruton, Roger 36, 42–9, 53–4, 76,
    175
Sixth Sense, The (Shyamalan) 61–4
security 2, 12–13, 149–50
September 11 see 11 September 2001
Shyamalan, M Knight see Sixth Sense,
    The
social contract 47–8
Solon 5
Somalia 40
Sophocles see Antigone
Souter, Justice David 159–60
South Africa 71, 73–4
South Korea 71, 170–1
sovereignty 4–5, 7, 25–6, 29–30,
    132–3, 134, 136–7, 146–50

Spanish–American War (1898)
    124–7
Spengler, Oswald 27
Stevens, Justice John Paul 151,
    156–7, 160–1
Stiegler, Bernard 178
"Stolen generation," the 64–8,
    77–8
Strauss, Leo 27–8, 29, 30, 36, 174

Tampa incident 113–23, 152
terrorism 19, 37, 42, 129–30, 140, 149
Thomas, Justice Clarence 160
time 51–2, 80–1, 166
torture 142, 143, 151, 155–6, 157,
    163, 164–5, 167–70, 177
trauma 165–8

United States of America 12, 14–35,
    48–50, 71, 89–91, 94, 110,
    124–30, 134, 137–49, 152–3,
    155–63, 162–3, 170
universalism 44–5, 106–7

Vardalis, Eric 115
Vernant, Jean-Pierre 43
Vietnam 9, 39
violence 1–3, 6–9, 12, 52, 78–9, 138,
    151–2, 170–3
von Trier, Lars see Epidemic

Wannsee conference 10, 141
war 9, 12–13, 36–8, 131–8
"War on Terror," the 1–3, 140,
    148–9, 155–6, 159–62, 164
Weimar republic 51–2, 136
Weyler y Nicolau, Valeriano 125–6
Whitlam, Gough 91
Wilkinson, Marian see Dark Victory
Windeyer, Justice Victor 104
Wolfowitz, Paul 20–1, 23–5, 26–30,
    31–2, 33, 34, 35, 36, 39
World War II 135, 140, 147